GUITAR TAPPING

by Chad Johnson

To access audio visit:
www.halleonard.com/mylibrary

Enter Code
2022-6232-2014-4464

ISBN 978-0-634-04647-6

HAL•LEONARD® CORPORATION

7777 W. BLUEMOUND RD. P.O. BOX 13819 MILWAUKEE, WI 53213

Visit Hal Leonard Online at
www.halleonard.com

Table of Contents

Introduction

In 1978, an instrumental guitar solo featured on the self-titled debut album of California hard-rock/heavy-metal band Van Halen turned the rock guitar world on its ear, almost instantly. The track had guitar players the world over scratching their heads in disbelief at what they heard. The level of flash and speed displayed on the tune "Eruption" was totally unprecedented in the world of rock guitar, and guitarist Eddie Van Halen was aware that he was onto something big. During his solo on stage in the early days, Eddie would reportedly turn his back to the audience as to not reveal his new secret weapon. That secret weapon was tapping. While it's unclear as to who actually invented the technique, it is certainly clear that Eddie Van Halen is responsible for starting the tapping phenomenon. It wasn't too long before the cat was out of the bag, and guitar players everywhere soon added the technique to their own bag of tricks. By the mid eighties, you couldn't walk into a guitar store without hearing a tapping lick.

Throughout the eighties, many rock players modified and expanded tapping to suit their own unique styles, and the true potential of the technique began to be realized. Steve Vai, Reb Beach (of Winger), and Joe Satriani all made extensive use of tapping in their styles, each achieving unique results. Jeff Watson (of Night Ranger) became known for his eight-fingered tapping technique, while Vito Bratta (of White Lion) applied an extremely melodic approach to the style, demonstrating that this technique was capable of more than just flash. Jazz/rock/fusion player Jennifer Batten took the eight-fingered technique seemingly to the limit, all but getting rid of her pick altogether, while steel-string master Michael Hedges applied the technique to his acoustic style with a uniqueness that had to be heard to be believed. Meanwhile, jazz guitarist Stanley Jordan went off the deep end, creating a truly bi-dextral style of tapping chords with the left hand while tapping melodies with the right.

The applications of the tapping technique are far-reaching to say the least. In this book, we'll take a detailed look at the technique and many of its more common variations. Hopefully by the end you'll have gained a more thorough understanding of the technique and a new appreciation for its nearly boundless potential.

How to Use This Book

Each chapter in this book covers a different aspect or application of tapping technique and includes exercises and licks to help you become familiar with the aspect introduced. While the exercises, somewhat predictable and academic in nature, are designed to familiarize you with a specific technique, feel free to use them as licks as well. Many times, they'll spark an idea that can be tweaked into a great-sounding lick. At the end of most chapters, a section entitled Style Applications will demonstrate these concepts in a full band setting, allowing you to hear how these ideas can be applied to actual musical situations in several different styles.

About the Audio

On the accompanying audio tracks, each example is played three times: once at a medium tempo, once at a faster tempo, and once at a slow tempo for closer examination. For the Style Applications tracks, the featured guitar parts are panned hard right, while the rhythm instruments are panned hard left. By adjusting the balance control on your stereo or computer, you can completely remove the featured guitar part, allowing you to play over the backing tracks yourself. You can also single out the featured guitar part for closer scrutiny. Track 85 contains tuning notes for reference.

Guitars: Chad Johnson
Drums: Lance Ogletree
Bass: Erik Shieffer
Recorded at Famous Beagle Studios in Plano, TX

1 The Basics

The technique of two-hand tapping is essentially an extension of left-hand legato technique—A finger from the right hand is used as an extra fret-hand finger, if you will, opening a whole new world of possibilities. In this chapter we're going to look at the most basic applications of this technique; the good thing about these exercises and licks is that, in just a few hours, you can sound like a pro. It doesn't take long to get the hang of the technique. The remaining chapters will take a bit longer to work up to speed. It should be noted that most rock players generally use a fair amount of gain when tapping, but the technique can be used with virtually any guitar setup. Also remember to expect some soreness if this is your first time tapping. Your right-hand finger is going to need to develop a callous, just as your left-hand fingers did when you first started playing. Let's get on with it.

Some Notes on the Right Hand

Due to the fact that a fair amount of gain is often used when tapping, it's important to develop a solid muting technique. Otherwise, the low strings (usually kept quiet by the palm of your right hand) will begin to ring undesirably. Effective muting is achieved by anchoring your right hand with your thumb along the top of the neck and allowing your palm to deaden the strings that aren't being played (see photo at right).

Some players prefer to use their first finger to tap, and some use their second. If you use your first, you'll need to do something with your pick. Most players prefer to slip the pick over to their second finger, holding it between the two knuckles or against the palm (see left photo). Alternatively, some players will just hold the pick in between their lips. Experiment and see which works best for you. Just remember that you need to be swift about it, whichever method you choose; many times you'll be required to move from picking to tapping and back fairly quickly.

Exercise #1

In Exercise #1, we see one of the most common tapping patterns of all. This triplet figure forms an E minor arpeggio and is played entirely on the B string. If you're not entirely familiar with arpeggios and their construction, we'll take a closer look at them in Chapter 2. To perform the pattern, begin by planting your left-hand first finger on the E note at the fifth fret. Now, with either the first or second finger of your right hand, tap the B note on the twelfth fret and pull it off to the E note. Finish off by hammering onto the G note at the eighth fret with your left-hand pinky (or ring finger if you prefer). As you tap the B note again to repeat the pattern, remember to lift your left-hand finger off the G note, leaving the first finger planted on the E note below.

TRACK 1

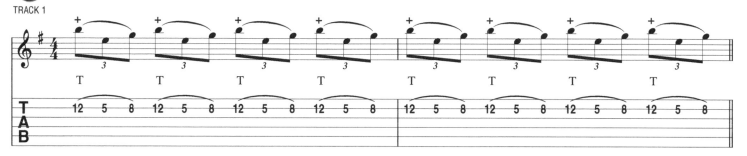

Exercise #2

Exercise #2 simply reverses the left-hand notes. You'll need to begin by planting your pinky on the G note and your first finger on the E note. Tap the B note and pull off to the G, then pull the G off to the E. While repeating this sequence, the most difficult part will be planting your pinky on the G note after you tap the B and before you pull it off. If you try to plant the G too soon, you will sound the note. It needs to be planted just after the B note is tapped.

TRACK 2

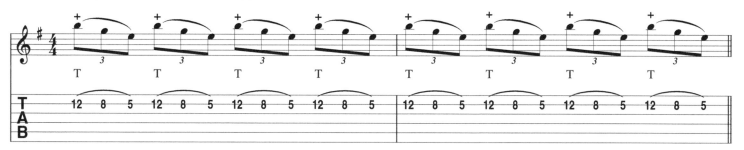

Exercise #3

Here we're combining Exercises 1 and 2 into one pattern. Because of this alternation, you won't really need to worry about planting your fingers. For example, after hammering onto the G note at the end of beat 1, you can simply keep your pinky there since you're going to be pulling off the B note to it anyway. This type of pattern sounds really interesting when sped up.

TRACK 3

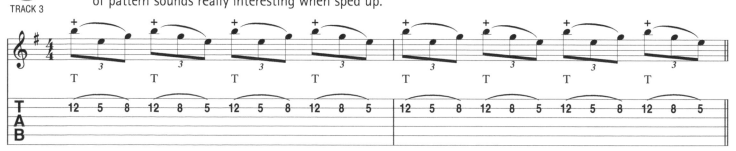

Lick #1

In this lick, we tap through the progression of Em–C–D–Em using the pattern from Exercise #1. We begin in measure 1 with the original arpeggio, Em. In measure 2, we move our tapping note one half step up to C. In measure 3, we shift the whole shape up one whole step to D. We finish in measure 4 with an E minor arpeggio featuring a major 3rd shape in our fret hand. If you'd been using your ring finger thus far, this would be a good time to bring in your pinky. Notice also that the final tapped E note is treated to vibrato. When adding vibrato to a tapped note, most players will usually vibrato the string as normal with a left-hand finger below and let the tapped note just hang on for the ride. In this example, for instance, I would vibrato the string with my left-hand pinky, since it was the last finger used before the tapped note. You will hear the vibrato on the E note, even though you're not moving your right hand. NOTE: this technique works best with the vertical rock-style vibrato. It's very subtle if used with the horizontal classical-style.

TRACK 4

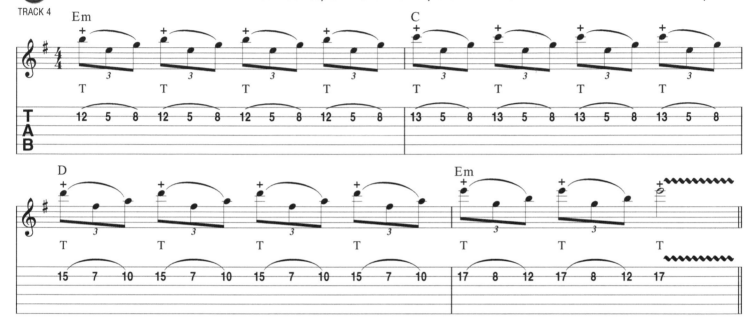

Lick #2

Lick #2, based off the alternating pattern of Exercise #3, moves through the progression of D–Dmaj7–D7–G–Gm–D–A7–D entirely on the G string. Notice that, in measures 1–3, the only movement needed is the lowering of the tapped note by half steps. In measures 4 and 5, you'll need to stretch quite a bit in the left hand from the D to the G.

TRACK 5

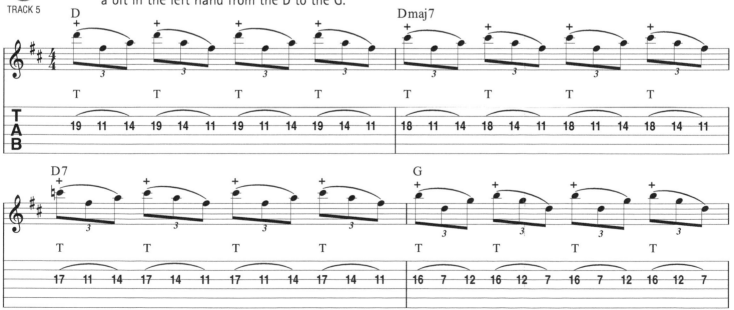

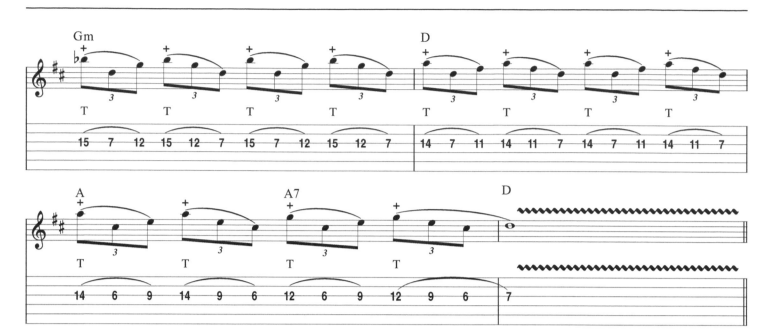

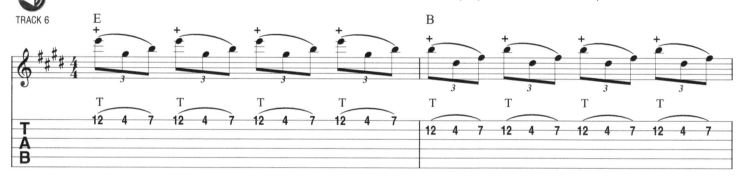

Lick #3

Here we move through a common classical progression in E using the top two strings. Several important concepts should be noted here. First, note the use of similar shapes transposed for different chords. The E, B, and A chords, for instance, all use the same shape. Next, note the use of a *common tone* (G#) between the C#m and G#m chords. This is a common classical device that provides a smooth transition between the chords. Finally, note the use of open strings in measures 4 (G#m) and 6 (E). Open strings, when the key signature permits, sound very nice when used in conjunction with tapped notes. They also provide a nice opportunity to make a shift with the left hand if need be to prepare for another shape.

TRACK 6

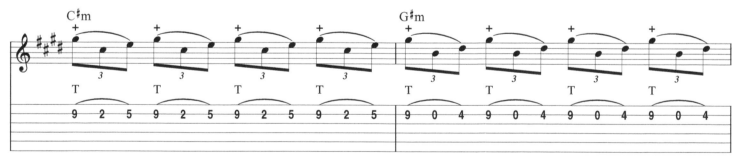

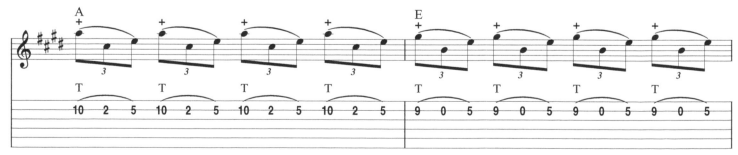

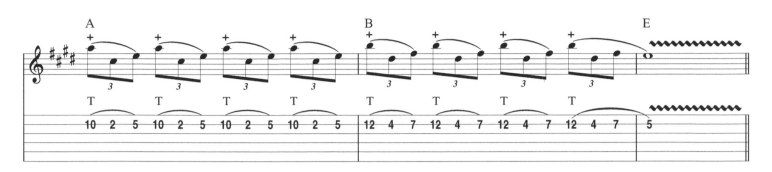

Lick #4

Lick #4 makes use of open strings extensively, using the B and E strings as pedal points to define the passing chords. Measures 1 and 3 make use of common tones as well as imitative phrasing. In measure 5, another classical device, *contrary motion,* is used to outline the progression of E–F#7–Amaj7. Note that the tapped note ascends in whole steps while the left hand descends in half steps.

TRACK 7

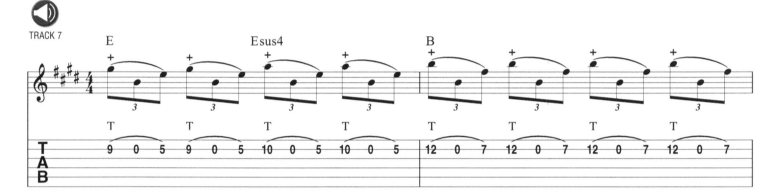

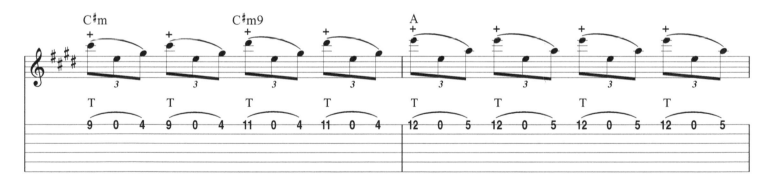

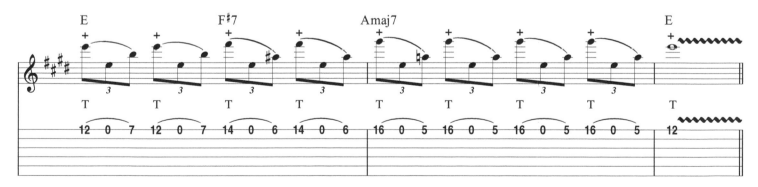

Arpeggios

You may have noticed that we dealt with arpeggios in Chapter 1 a bit already. This is because arpeggios are the most common application of tapping technique and are therefore a great way to introduce the technique. In this chapter, we're going to take a closer look at arpeggios and what we can do with them.

First of all, an *arpeggio* is simply the notes of a chord played separately, one at a time. The notes can be played in any order: ascending, descending, or in any combination. Let's take a look at a C major triad as an example.

First let's look at some of the possible ways to play this arpeggio using a traditional left-hand technique:

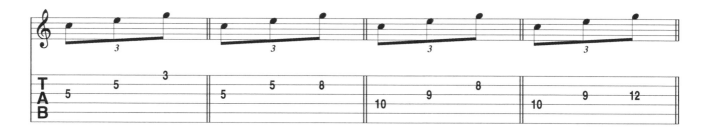

And now let's see how we could employ tapping to play the arpeggio:

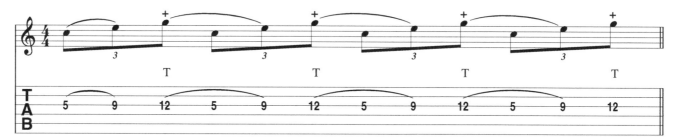

You can probably now understand why tapping is commonly applied to arpeggios. You can fly through them with minimal effort. You may need to stretch a bit in your left hand to accommodate some of the shapes, but once you get used to this, it's a breeze.

A Note on Rhythm

There is one important thing to watch when tapping that is many times overlooked: the placement of the accent. It's very easy, for instance, for example A below to end up sounding like example B if you're not careful:

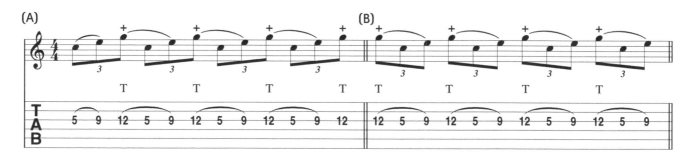

You'll need to really listen closely and make sure that you're placing the accent where it needs to be. It's probably easiest to perform tapping licks in which the tapped note falls on the downbeat, and many players will get into the habit of only playing this type of tapping lick. But, as seen in the previous example, other rhythms are possible as well. It's important to be able to use the tapping technique in any rhythmical situation. Here's a great exercise for applying different rhythms to the same three-note tapping lick. It's very important to use a metronome for this exercise, as it will make sure you're hearing the beat properly against the lick.

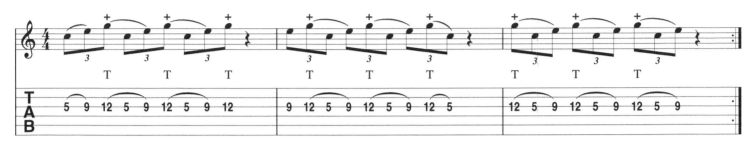

Exercise #1

In this first arpeggio exercise, we're moving across all six strings through different inversions of an E major triad. An *inversion* is simply a chord played with a note other than the root on the bottom. An E major triad is spelled E–G♯–B. This is known as "root position." If we were to transpose the lowest note (the root E) up one octave, we would end up with G♯–B–E. This is known as "first inversion." If we were to repeat the process again and transpose the lowest note (G♯) up an octave, we would now have B–E–G♯, or "second inversion." Repeating the process again would put us back in root position. In this exercise, we'll see each inversion twice.

Moving up through the six strings, the shapes are: first inversion, second inversion, root position, first inversion, second inversion, and root position. In measure 2, you'll have a big stretch for the second inversion shape. Second inversion shapes of triads usually will require a stretch because of the 4th interval between the 5th and root of the chord. We get around this stretch in measure 5 with the use of the open string.

TRACK 8

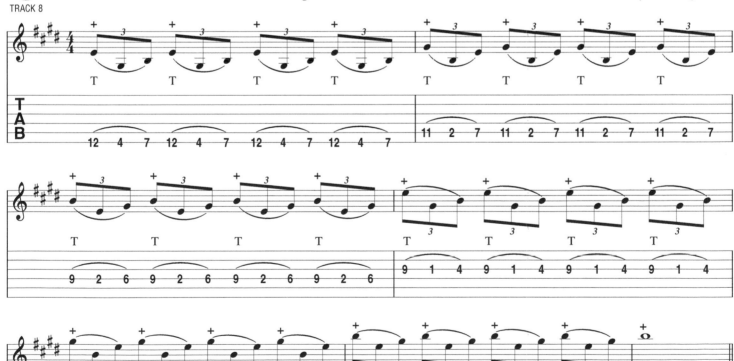

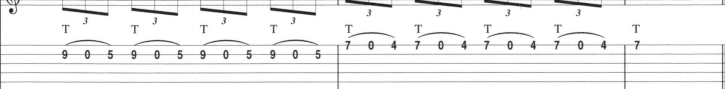

Exercise #2

In Exercise #2 we see the same concept applied to an Em arpeggio through all six strings.

Exercise #3

In Exercise #3, we take the first inversion shape and ascend through all the diatonic chords from E major. This linear approach will be a bit harder to master than the vertical approach from the previous exercises. Measures 6–10 repeat the same thing an octave higher.

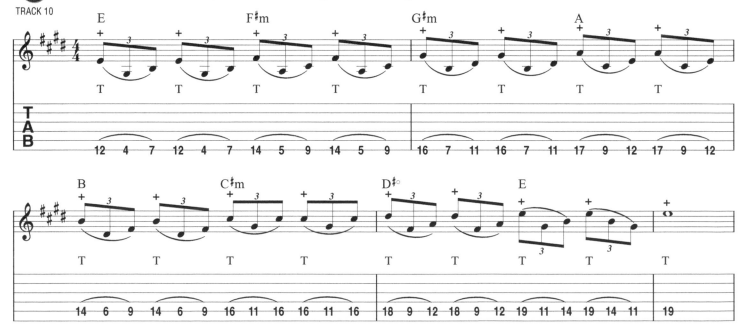

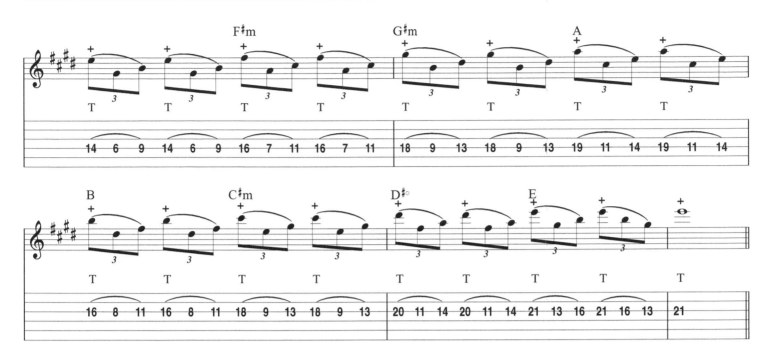

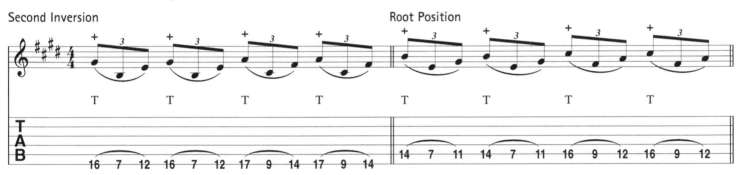

As an important variation to this exercise, move through the chords using the root position and second inversion shapes. I'll start you off below with a few of each.

Exercise #4

Here we see the descending version of Exercise #3. The string groups have to be modified a little bit to accommodate for the open strings.

TRACK 11

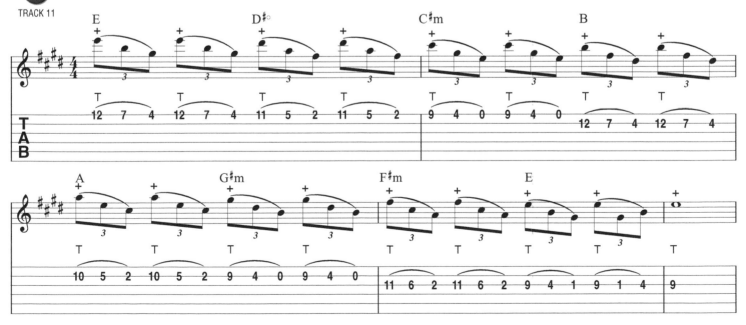

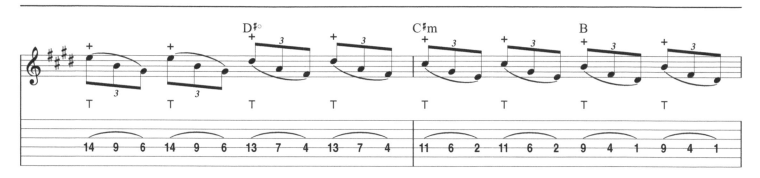

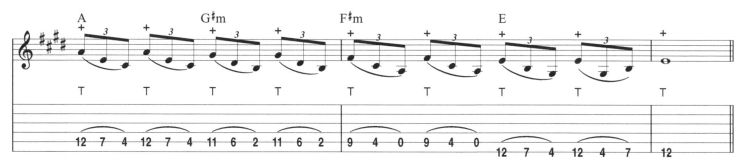

Lick #1

TRACK 12

In this first lick, played entirely on the B string, we create a bit of syncopation by playing the three-note arpeggio in a sixteenth-note rhythm. The rhythm exercise you practiced earlier will pay off here. Make sure you don't hammer on with your left hand after each third tapped note. This two-note abbreviated figure is what gets you back on beat for each new arpeggio.

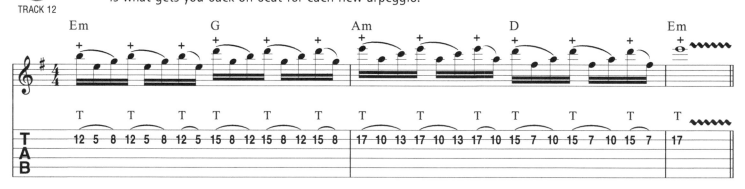

Lick #2

TRACK 13

In this A harmonic minor lick, we exploit the open E string as a common tone between the Am and E7 chords. As a variation on this lick, try tapping through all the arpeggios in Am with this open-string sixteenth-note pattern.

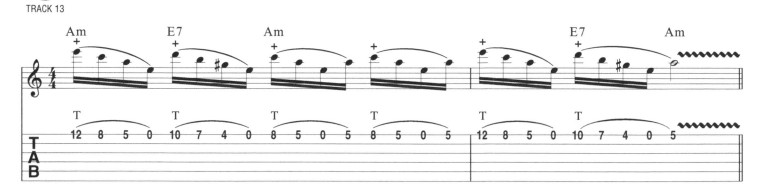

Lick #3

Here we see a progression in B major played on the B string. Notice that the open B string is included at the end of measures 2 and 4. Beats 3 in measures 2 and 4 will require a bit of a stretch.

TRACK 14

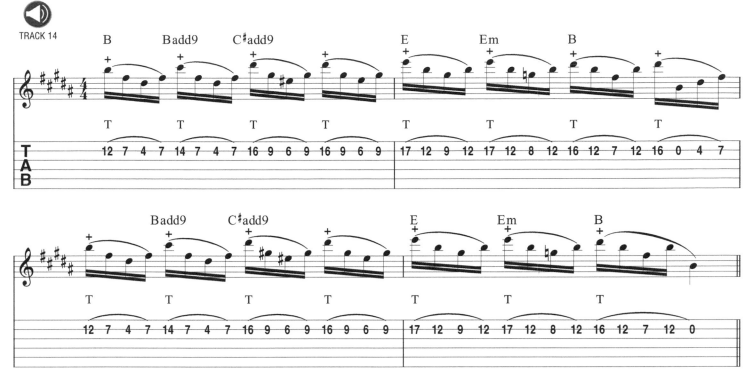

Lick #4

Lick #4, in G major, takes place entirely on the G string and features many quick position shifts, so take it slowly at first. In measure 4, you'll need to shift your left hand down a 4th from the C shape to the G shape, with your pinky (or third finger) guiding the shift, since it is immediately pulled off to from the tapped B note on beat 3.

TRACK 15

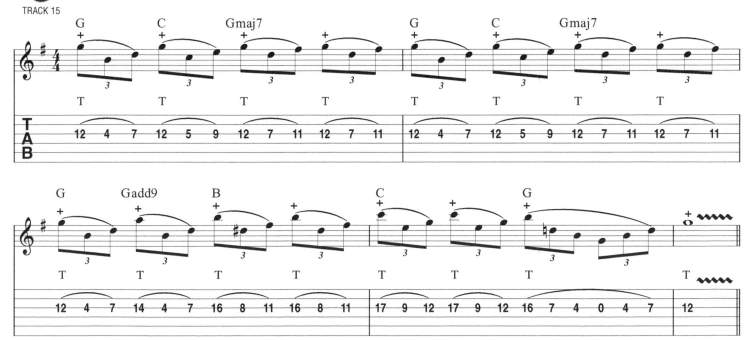

Style Applications

Rock

Here we see a sequenced idea over a V–I progression in G major. Notice the pattern of the tapped notes, which repeats every half-measure. Your tapping hand will stay pretty active here, but your left hand really only has to make one shift at the beginning of measure 2.

TRACK 16

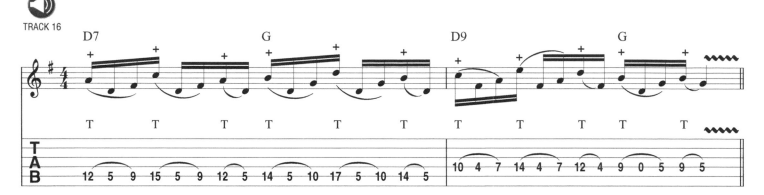

Metal

This metal lick is a classic example of the technique being put to use for good ol' fashioned flash. Again, your left hand remains pretty stationary here, while the tapped notes take care of the melody. Note the use of the F♯ in measure 1, derived from the G harmonic minor scale.

TRACK 17

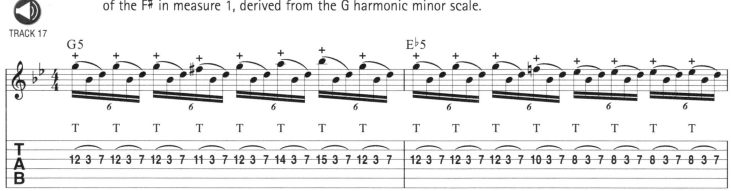

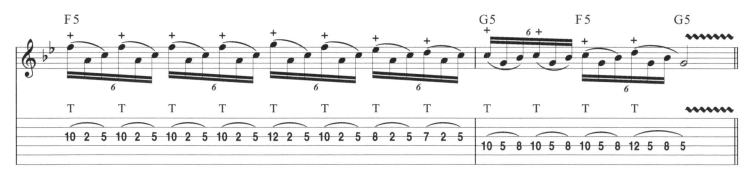

Rock

Here we see a sparser, more melodic approach. Notice that the exact same major shape is moved up on the G string from the I chord (C) to the II chord (D); the only difference is the ending note. This helps to keep the phrase from sounding too predictable and stale. This creates a descending melody, E–D, which is resolved at the end of the next arpeggio (F) with the note C. Although this is an octave higher, the listener will still infer the feeling of resolution. After this shape is moved up a whole step for the G chord, the phrase wraps up with a skipped string.

TRACK 18

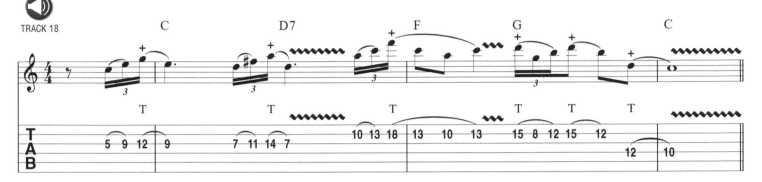

Country

This pseudo-country lick takes place entirely on the B string. In this I–II–IV–I progression, the E7 pattern from measure 1 is slid up and repeated verbatim over the F#7 chord in measure 2. We then slide down a half step to resolve into the A chord in measure 3 with a slightly different pattern. In measure 4, we end up back where we started for the E chord and wrap things up with a bluesy G♮–G# slide.

TRACK 19

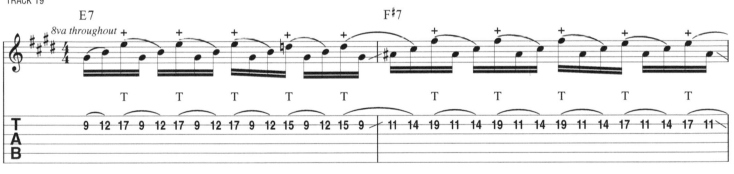

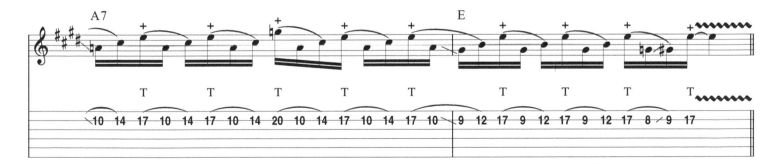

3 Scale Fragments

In the previous chapter, you may have noticed that we focused entirely on three-note groups. That is to say, we always had one tapped note and two different fret-hand notes. (One of the fret-hand notes may have been repeated, creating a four-note group, but there were still only three different notes.) In this chapter, we're going to include more notes in our fretting hand to expand our possibilities a bit. I used the term "scale fragments" because we are essentially playing a fragment of a scale by doing this, but this not to say that you can't mix in arpeggios as well. This chapter is simply removing the limitations we had in the arpeggio chapter.

Exercise #1

In this first exercise, we tap through the notes of a descending C major scale. Because of the particular shape we're using, we have a repeated note at the beginning of every beat. This can really provide a unique effect when played at faster tempos. For an interesting variation on this pattern, try beginning on the "and" of beat 1 instead of the downbeat.

TRACK 20

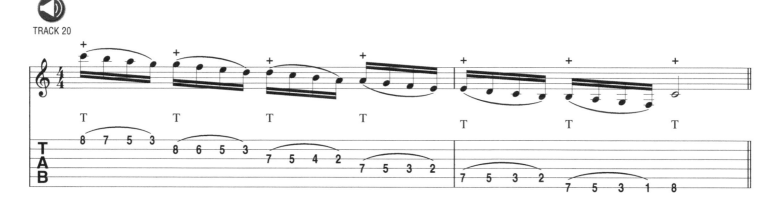

Exercise #2

This example is based on slightly altering the order of the notes in Exercise #1. Because of the altered pattern, the repeated note won't really be perceived as such here.

TRACK 21

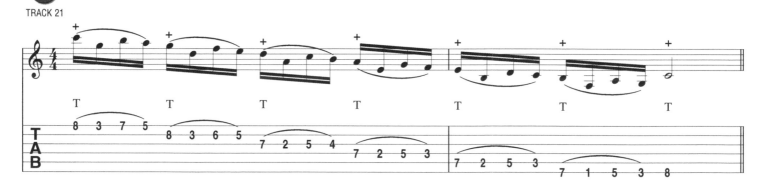

Exercise #3

Exercise #3 repeats an A major pattern in three octaves and features alternating melodic direction on each string. On beat 4, you'll be forced to quickly shift your pinky from the G# on string 4 to the D on string 3. This process is repeated an octave higher in measure 2. Take your time and make sure you're getting this cleanly before raising the tempo.

TRACK 22

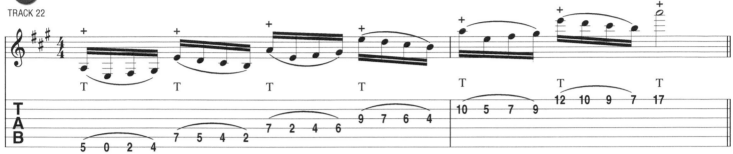

Exercise #4

Exercise #4 is one of those exercises that makes a pretty cool lick as well. Here we see a G minor pentatonic pattern repeated in two octaves. At the end of beats 1, 2, and 3, you'll be required to perform a "hammer-on from nowhere" with your left hand. The most difficult aspect of this technique is timing the release of one note with the hammer-on of the new note. You don't want the notes to ring together, but you don't want to hear a gap between them either. I've included a left-hand fingering that works best for me.

TRACK 23

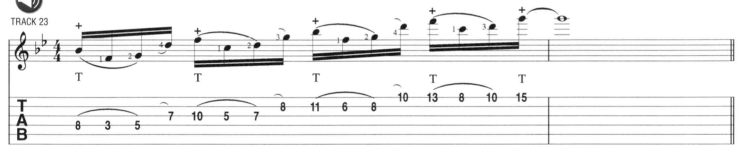

Lick #1

Here we see a D minor lick that uses a pattern of six notes in a sixteenth-note rhythm. We begin with a line based off the D minor scale on the G string. Notice that in beat 4 of each measure the abbreviated four-note pattern sets up the next measure. In measure 2, you'll only need to raise your tapping note one half step. In measure 3, we move up to the B string for a line that hints at F major. In beat 4, the C note is raised to C#, implying an A7 tonality, before the line resolves in measure 4 with the high D note.

TRACK 24

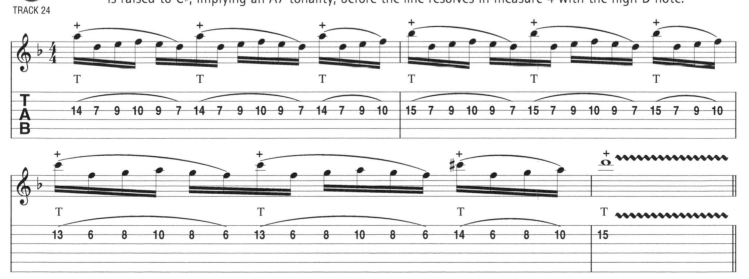

Lick #2

Lick #2 is based off a descending Gmaj7 arpeggio sequence. The first and second notes of each beat arpeggiate the notes of Gmaj7, while the third and fourth notes of each beat fill the line in with stepwise motion. Try flatting F# to F♮ for an interesting dominant 7th variation.

TRACK 25

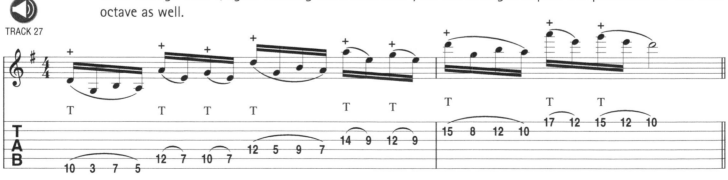

Lick #3

In Lick #3 we find a sequence based off an A major scale. With a sextuplet pattern built off each note in the scale, we ascend through an entire octave. The only variation in the pattern comes in beat 4 of measure 1; here you'll use only four notes and alter melodic direction for a mid-lick breather before moving up to the first string to tackle the second half.

TRACK 26

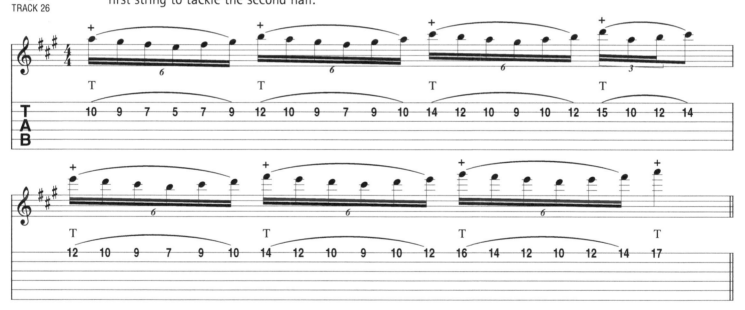

Lick #4

Lick #4 is based off a repeating E minor pentatonic pattern in three octaves. Your tapping hand will double up every other beat in this one. To avoid unnecessary shifting, try this: remain in third position for beats 1 and 2, catching the E note in beat 2 with your fourth finger. Shift on beat 3 to fifth position and remain there through beat 4, again catching the E note with your fourth finger. Repeat this procedure for the final octave as well.

TRACK 27

Style Applications

Hard Rock

Here we find a very typical hard rock approach. We begin in measure 1 with an E minor pattern featuring an alternating tapped note and alternating melodic direction for each beat. This basic pattern is moved up to fit each chord in the progression. Notice that measure 3 is simply measure 2 transposed up a whole step. The most difficult aspect of this lick will most likely be the beginning of measures 2 and 4. Here you'll be required to quickly shift your first finger to a new string and be ready for the pull off from the tapped note. Practice this move slowly and gradually build up speed.

TRACK 28

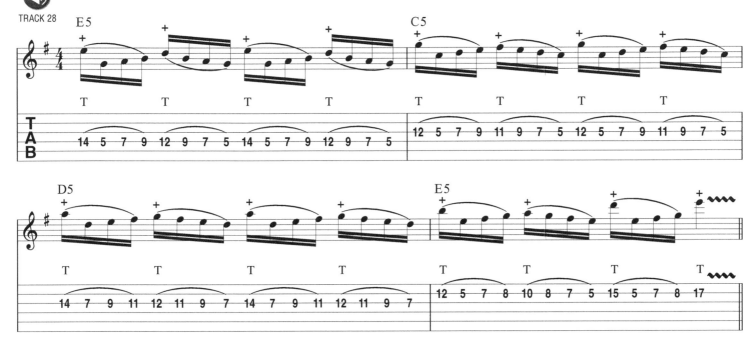

Fusion

In this lick we find a more angular melodic approach. In measure 1 (first complete measure) we find an interesting situation. After tapping the C♯ on beat 1, we tap the B on beat 2 with no pull-off between the notes. In order to achieve this, simply deaden the strings with your left hand while holding the tapped C♯ on beat 1. This way, you can quickly move your tapping finger from C♯ to B with no noise between the notes. In measure 2, after an eighth-note phrase implying A–C♯7, you'll need to shift your fourth finger down to the ninth fret to get in position for the quick, bluesy scalar descent. For the final F♯, we skip the B string and tap the note on the G string.

TRACK 29

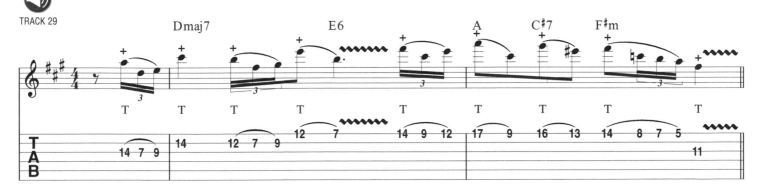

Rock

Here we find another melodic approach over a D minor progression. After a quick pick-up flurry, we find a syncopated melody played on the B string through beat 3. On beat 4, we tap through an A minor pentatonic phrase, sustaining the E note over the bar line to create an Fmaj7 tonality. More syncopation follows in measure 2, and we close things out in beat 3 with a quick descending scale fragment. (Note: the A note in beat 3 of measure 2 could easily be handled by the left hand, but I chose to tap it for the reason of consistency in tone. If you prefer to use your left hand here, go for it.)

TRACK 30

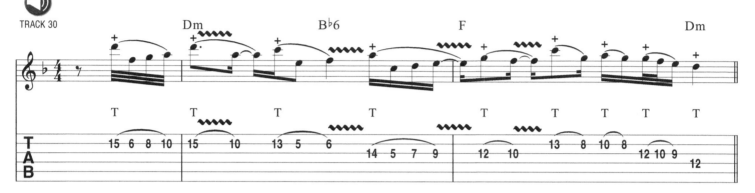

Metal

This lick gets back to the flash factor. Over some stop-time power chords in C minor, we tap through a pattern closely based on Lick #1 in this section. As most of this lick is performed on the high E string, it shouldn't pose too much of a problem. Be careful of the shift in beat 4 of measure 3; make sure it's clean and each note is heard clearly.

TRACK 31

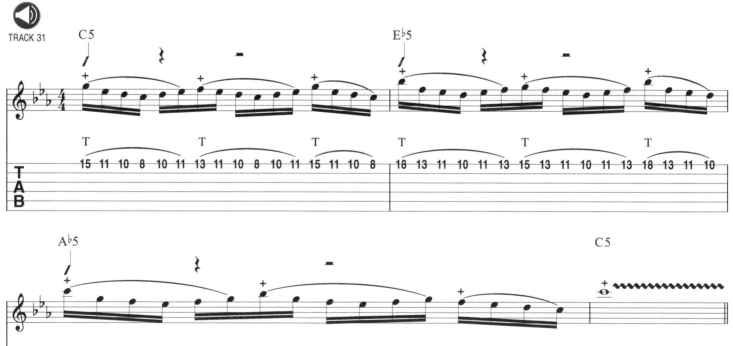

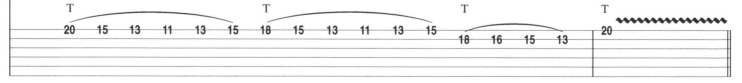

4 The Ascending Tap Concept

Thus far in this book, each time a left-hand note followed a tapped note, the left-hand note always fell on the same string as the tapped note and therefore below in pitch. It is possible to use tapping in another fashion as well, though. I call this the *ascending tap concept.* In this method of tapping, the left-hand note following the tapped note will fall on a higher string and (usually) be *above* in pitch. With this concept, four-note-per-string scales are possible as well as a myriad of other arpeggio and scalar applications.

Exercise #1

We'll begin in Exercise #1 here with a G major scale in three full octaves. In this exercise, we ascend through the scale with four notes on each string, gracefully gliding across the fretboard. For the first G note, you have a few options: 1) attack the note with your pick and then palm it for the rest of the lick, 2) set it in motion by silently pulling off from one of your left-hand fingers, or 3) set it in motion by silently pulling off from your tapping finger at the eight fret. I prefer the latter of these; I won't have to worry about palming my pick in the middle of the lick, and it puts me in position already to tap the C note.

For the D note on beat 3, you have two options: 1) you can "hammer on from nowhere" with your left-hand first finger, or 2) you can use your second or third right-hand finger to "pluck" the string to set it in motion. (Obviously, your second finger is not a possibility here if you use it as your primary tapping finger.)

TRACK 32

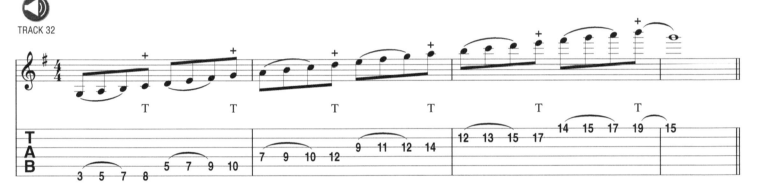

There are advantages to both methods of attacking the new string. Hammering on with your left hand provides a consistent tone and is pretty much a no-brainer. However, this technique is more difficult to achieve with less gain, whereas the plucking technique works well either way. I find myself employing both methods from time to time, but I tend to use the plucking method more often because it seems to divide the labor between the two hands nicely. Throughout the remaining of this book, the notation will not in- dicate either method, as both should be experimented with ideally. If you choose to employ the plucking method, here's a tip: try to get into the habit of placing your second finger (or third if you prefer) of your right hand at the same as your tapping finger. In other words, in beat 2 of the above example, as I tap the C note on the eighth fret, I will simultaneously place my second finger on the fifth string (at around the ninth fret) in preparation for the plucking of the D note. This will greatly aid the process when speeding things up.

Exercise #2

Exercise #2 repeats a four-note G major pentatonic figure in three octaves. If you're plucking the new string on this one, you may find it easier to use the third finger of your right hand instead of the second because of the skipped string. Either one is possible, however.

TRACK 33

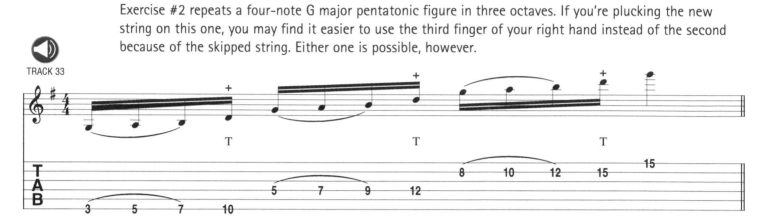

Exercise #3

Here we see an ascending A minor scale figure repeated in octaves featuring a repeated D note. The interesting thing about this pattern is that the hands alternating shifting positions, so your eyes will have to move back and forth each beat until you get the feel of the shifts.

TRACK 34

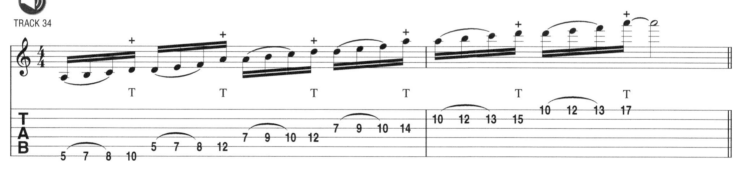

Exercise #4

Exercise #4 climbs up a three-octave A major arpeggio. This may take a while to get the shifting down, but when you realize that you're just shifting the same shape up to each new string, it will start to fall into place. You should try this example with these other triads as well: Am (A–C–E), A° (A–C–E♭), A+ (A–C#–F), Asus4 (A–D–E), and Asus2 (A–B–E).

TRACK 35

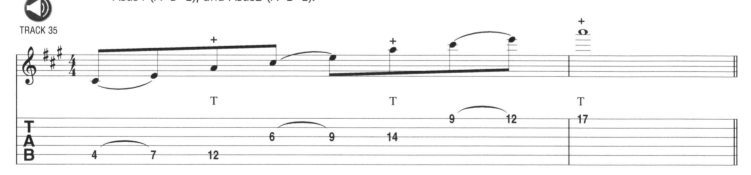

Exercise #5

Exercise #5 builds upon #4 by creating a major 7th arpeggio. This time in G, we include the 7th by way of sliding our first finger from F# to G. Again, try these other 7th chords with this exercise: Gm7 (G–Bb–D–F), G7 (G–B–D–F), G°7 (G–Bb–Db–E), G+7 (G–B–D#–F), and Gm(maj7) (G–Bb–D–F#).

TRACK 36

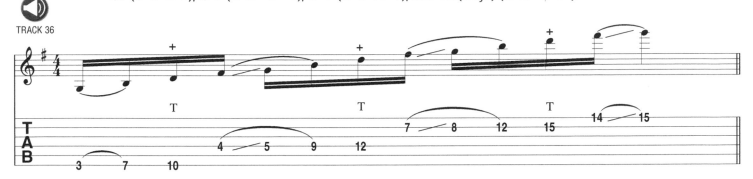

Exercise #6

Here we find a C minor arpeggio pattern that ascends *and* descends. You'll be forced to tap, ascend to a new string, and then tap the same note directly again. This may take a little time to get used to, but practice it slowly first and you'll get the feel of it. In beat 1 of measure 2, you may want to use your left-hand third finger to hammer the Eb note so your fourth finger can catch the C note on the high E string. This way, the same finger won't have to jump all over the place.

TRACK 37

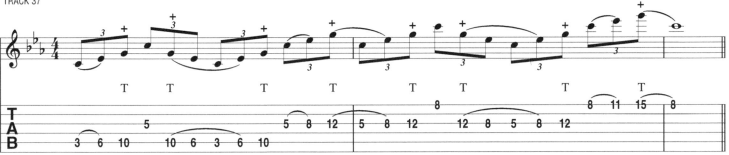

Exercise #7

Our final ascending tap exercise is built off a G major arpeggio pattern repeated in ascending octaves. At the end of each two-beat pattern, a bluesy Bb is slid up into B♮ to start the pattern over in the next octave. In beat 2 of measure 2, you'll be required to slide your fourth finger from the D up to the G in the space of one sixteenth note.

TRACK 38

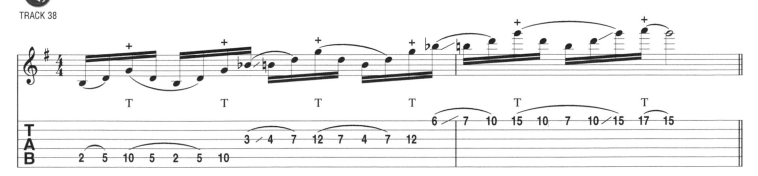

Lick #1

Our first lick comes from the E minor scale. We begin in beats 1 and 2 by repeating a four-note fragment an octave higher. In beat 3, we see a somewhat rare occurrence of the ascending tap technique used in conjunction with a *lower* pitch. This fragment in beat 3 is the same fragment from the first two beats transposed up a 4th. Beat 4 finds us again lower in pitch than the previous tapped note with a new fragment to resolve on the final E note.

TRACK 39

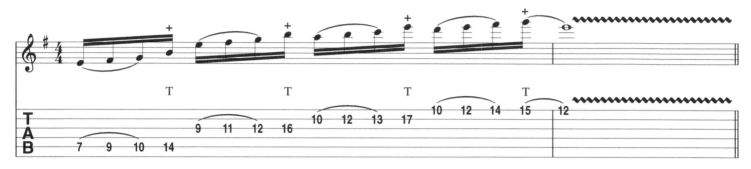

Lick #2

Lick #2 is built off a descending D minor scale and an ascending D harmonic minor scale. In beats 1 and 2, we descend through the natural minor scale on strings 1 and 2. We repeat this almost verbatim in beats 3 and 4 an octave lower; the only difference is in beat 4. Here we slide with our fourth finger from F to E, then pull off to C# to set up the next part of the lick. For measure 2, we slide up into D and continue up through a harmonic minor pattern in two octaves before resolving on the final D note in measure 3.

TRACK 40

Lick #3

In Lick #3, we're ascending through a pattern in F major repeated in octaves. The pattern begins in beat 1 with a pentatonic-based fragment and continues in beat 2 with a four-note ascent through notes of the major scale. This is repeated an octave higher, and we end on the 3rd (A) of the scale in measure 2.

TRACK 41

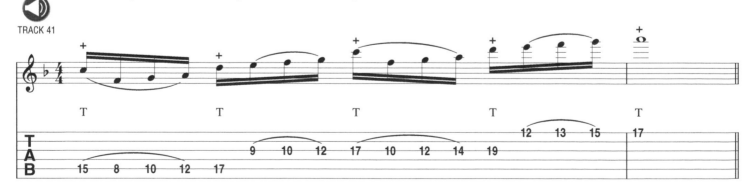

Lick #4

Lick #4 features a pattern played entirely on the fifth and third strings that's transposed through diatonic 7th chords in C. We begin in beat 1 by ascending through a C major triad and continue in beat 2 by descending through a Cmaj7 arpeggio. In beat 3, we slide up a whole step and see the Dm7 version of this pattern. Beats 1 and 2 of measure 2 contain our first C major pattern transposed to F major, and in beats 3 and 4 we slide up a whole step and alter the pattern slightly to fit the G7 chord. We finish off with a tapped C note in beat 3.

TRACK 42

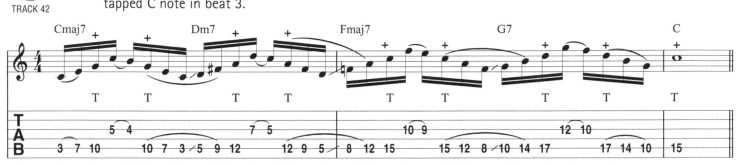

Style Applications

Up-Tempo Rock

Over an up-tempo rock feel in A minor, this lick begins with an ascending A minor scale fragment as a pickup. I use my third finger for the E note on the downbeat, as this sets me up in position for the rest of this measure nicely. In beat 3 of measure 2, you'll need to shift down a half step with your left hand for the B note, and in beat 4 you'll need to shift up to seventh position for the B note on the high E string. After hammering up to D and sliding that up to G, we finish off by tapping on the high A.

TRACK 43

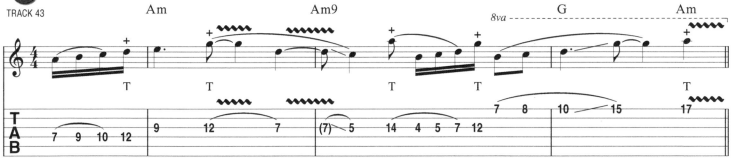

Slow Rock

This lick, in B major, features arpeggio-based phrases over a slow, steady rock groove. We begin with a B major arpeggio on string 5 that requires a shift in our tapping hand from the fourteenth to the ninth fret. This puts us in perfect position for the next E major arpeggio on string 4. For the E note at the end of this beat, I use my first finger to slide from E to D#. This will put you in position for the ascending B major arpeggio that follows. At the end of beat 3, you'll need to quickly shift your first finger from fifth position to ninth position to catch the C# note on the high E string. I use my third finger for the next D# note, and, while I'm tapping the following G# note, slide my third finger up to the fourteenth fret for the final F# note.

TRACK 44

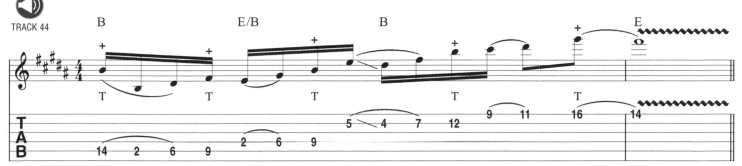

Jazz Fusion

In this lick, played over a jazz-fusion progression of Am7–D+7–Gmaj7, we begin by ascending through a fragment based on A minor. In beat 2, we imply an Am9 sound by including the B note. Beats 3 and 4 contain notes from the D whole tone scale (D–E–F#–G#–A#–C), a scale perfectly suited for the D+7 chord. We end in measure 2 by resolving to B, the 3rd of the Gmaj7 chord.

TRACK 45

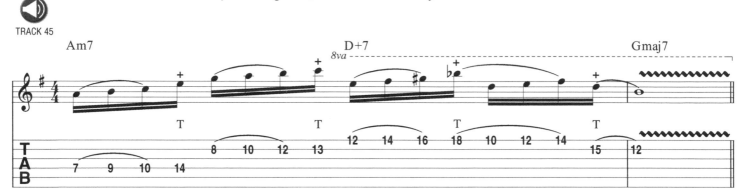

Fusion

Here we have a fusion-sounding lick in A minor that makes use of string skipping. The notes from beats 1 and 2 all fall within the A minor pentatonic scale. On beat 3, however, we hear a B note, implying Am9. In beat 4, we ascend up another pentatonic fragment and resolve on E, the 7th of Fmaj7.

TRACK 46

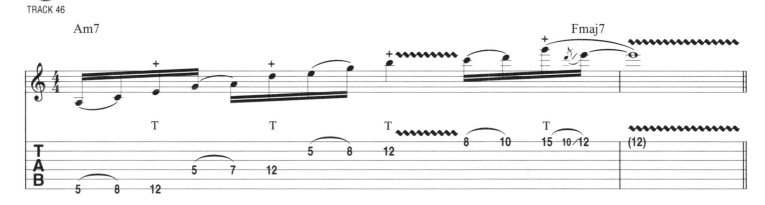

5 Additional Techniques

In this chapter, we'll deal with a few additional techniques that are commonly (and sometimes not so commonly) used in conjunction with tapping. They are: right-hand slides, tapped bends, tap harmonics, and chordal tapping. Each technique will be treated to its own exercises and licks, and the Style Applications section will feature one lick from each technique.

Right-Hand Slides

This technique is probably the easiest of all the additional techniques, so it's a good place to start. The idea is fairly self-explanatory; it involves tapping a note and then sliding to another note with that same right-hand tapping finger. Other than possibly digging a slightly larger groove into the tip of your tapping finger, the technique shouldn't be too much trouble.

Exercise #1

Since we just got off the subject of the ascending tap concept, why not combine our new tapped slides with it? In this example, we ascend through a C major scale with five notes per string. After tapping onto the F note, slide that finger up the G note before releasing it. On this type of ascending tap figure, the slide will give you more time to prepare for the plucked/hammered note on the new string; I find that this is actually easier to execute than the four-note-per-string ascending tap scales.

TRACK 47

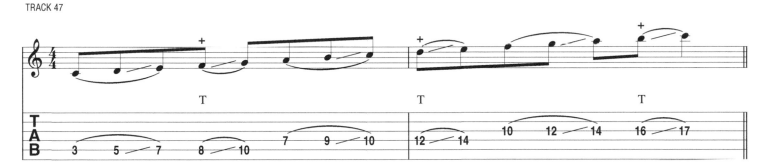

Exercise #2

Exercise #2 is built off a G7 arpeggio. We begin on the high E string by tapping the G note, sliding down to F, and pulling off for the D and B notes. This exact process is repeated an octave lower on the third string and again an octave lower on the fifth string. For the final G note on the sixth string, I hammer on with my left-hand second finger. For the first G and B notes in measure 2, you have some choices. You could use your left hand to hammer on the notes with your second and first fingers, respectively. Or you could do what I do: I use my right-hand thumb to pluck the low G note (at around the ninth fret) and my right-hand second finger to pluck the B note.

TRACK 48

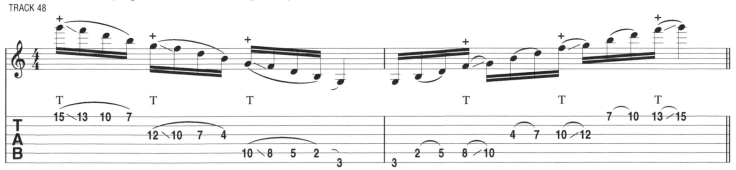

Lick #1

TRACK 49

Lick #1 is played entirely on the G string and is derived from the G major pentatonic scale. In beat 1, you'll need to shift your left hand into position for beat 2 while you're sliding the tapped G up to A. This process happens again in beat 2.

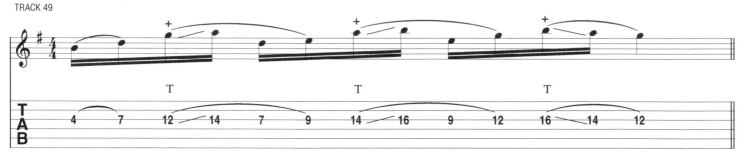

Lick #2

TRACK 50

In Lick #2, there's a lot of shifting, so learn it slowly. In beat 2, you'll have to shift your left hand down while sliding the tapped G to F♯, and again when sliding the tapped E to D in beat 3. For the E note in measure 2, you'll also either need to stretch or shift your left hand.

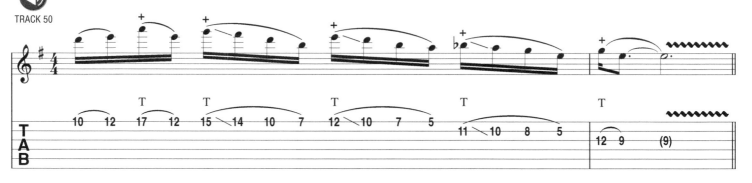

Tapped Bends

Just as there are many variations of the standard bending technique, there are several different variations to this technique as well. Most of them are commonly used, and all of them provide a unique and expressive sound. Here are some of the most common variations:

- The most obvious use is to tap a note and then, using your left hand, bend the note up to another pitch. It's very important that you use your left hand to do the bending. Just as in vibrato, the tapped note just hangs on for the ride. At this point, 1) the bend can be released, bringing the tapped note back down to its original pitch, or 2) the tapped note can be pulled off to the bent left-hand note below it.

- Alternatively, you can bend a note with your left hand and then tap onto a note while the string is still bent. You need to remember though that the tapped note is going to sound higher in pitch than the fret you're tapping because of the bend. At this point, the phrase can continue with either of the above-mentioned methods.

- You can also tap a pre-bent note and then continue with either of the above-mentioned methods. (To pre-bend a note, you silently bend the string the desired amount with your left hand first, before tapping onto the desired pitch.)

In the exercises and licks following, we'll see examples of all of these variations.

Exercise #1

In Exercise #1, based off a D major scale, we see an example of the most basic application of the technique. We begin by tapping the D note and bending it a whole step (with the left hand) up to E, releasing it down to D, and pulling off to the left hand below. In measure 2, we tap onto the E note and bend it up a whole step to F#, and release it again, pulling it off to the same left-hand fragment. In measure 3, we tap onto the F# note and bend it up a half step to G, release it again and pull it off. We then work our way back down the same way we came up.

TRACK 51

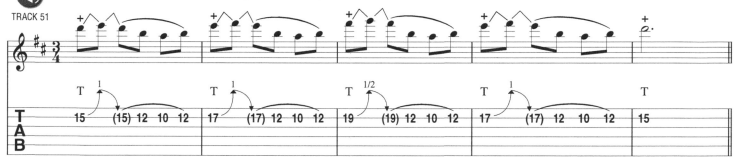

Exercise #2

In Exercise #2, we see the other two variations. First, pre-bend the B note on string 2 with your left-hand fourth (or third) finger a half step. Next tap onto the fourteenth fret, sounding the E note, release the bend to D#, and pull off to the B and G# in your left hand. On beat 3, slide the G# down to F# and hammer back up to A. Now, tap the C# and bend up a whole step to sound the D#—your left-hand finger should still be fretting the tenth fret holding the bend. Pull off the tapped note to the bent tenth fret, sounding a B note, and release the bend back to A. We finish things off by sliding down to D# and hammering onto E.

TRACK 52

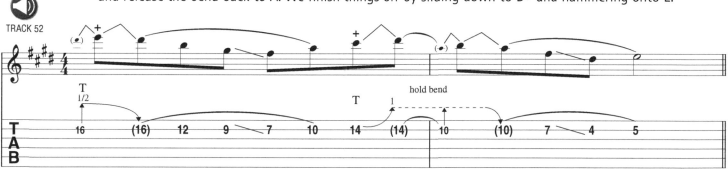

Lick #1

This first lick could just as easily be played in the B minor pentatonic box shape in seventh position. By using tapping, an entirely different tone is achieved. Begin by bending the E to F# with your third finger. Tap onto the fourteenth fret, sounding the B note, and release it down to A. While you're releasing the bend, you'll need to slide your third finger up to the eleventh fret for the F# note. The rest of the lick falls into place from there.

TRACK 53

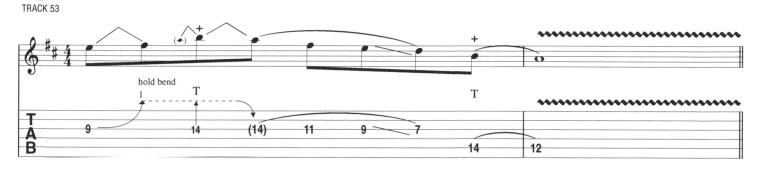

Lick #2

Lick #2 comes from the E blues scale. We begin on the second string by ascending up the to tapped D note, bending it up to E, releasing it back to D, and pulling off through which the same notes we ascended. Next, we shift down to the fourth string and tap/pull off a three-note fragment. This will put your left hand into position for the final bend. Here we tap the A note, bend it up a half step and release it, and pull it off to the G and E below.

TRACK 54

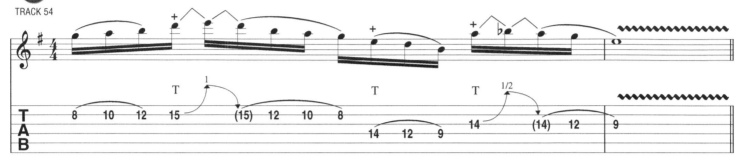

Tap Harmonics

The technique of tapping harmonics provides a unique timbre. It's a great way to set apart a specific melody, or just add punctuation at the end of a phrase. In the latter, it could be thought of as akin to a singer raising their voice an octave using falsetto on the last word of a phrase. Tapping harmonics will take a bit longer to get used to than the traditional harmonic technique, and it should be mentioned that, while normal tapping can be employed with little or no gain at all, tap harmonics usually require a decent amount of gain to get a clear, ringing tone.

Just as with natural harmonics, the technique of tapping harmonics works by dividing the length of the string in specific fractions, therefore producing certain different overtones depending upon the location of the tap.

To perform a tapped harmonic, play the lower fretted note (with either the pick or a hammer-on/pull-off), then, using your tapping finger, quickly tap (and immediately lift your finger off) the string directly above the fretwire (just as in a natural harmonic) at the indicated fret, causing the artificial harmonic to sound. Just as in natural harmonics, you'll find that certain harmonic points along the string will ring out much more easily than others, and a solid fret-hand muting technique is essential to assure the cleanest articulation.

Exercise #1

In this first exercise, we tap along various locations above the fretted C note, producing 5ths, octaves, and 3rds. We begin by playing the C note and then tapping a harmonic seven frets above at the twelfth fret. This produces a sounding note that is an octave plus a 5th higher than the fretted note. Next, we tap the tenth fret (five frets higher than the fretted note). This produces a note two octaves higher than the fretted note. After returning to the twelfth fret, we then tap nine frets higher than the fretted note at the fourteenth fret to sound an E note two octaves plus a major 3rd higher. It's back to the twelfth fret again, and then finally we tap the seventeenth fret (twelve frets higher) to sound the octave above the fretted note. This final harmonic will surely be the easiest to sound of all.

TRACK 55

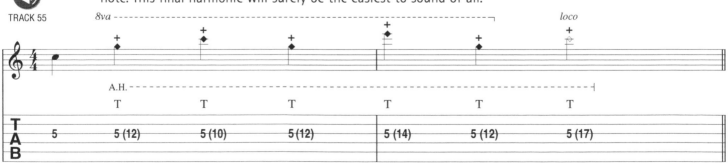

*A.H. = artificial harmonic

NOTE: This relationship of harmonic locations to sounding pitches will remain the same for any fretted note. In other words, tapping a harmonic at seven frets above a fretted note will always produce an octave plus a 5th above; tapping a harmonic twelve frets higher will always produce an octave above, etc.

Exercise #2

In Exercise #2, we're tapping harmonics exclusively, without even sounding a fretted note first. It may take a little bit of practice to separate your two hands. It may feel at first that your hands want to move together, but with slow and steady practice, this won't be a problem. This type of exercise demonstrates how fun it can be to experiment with tapped harmonics. Take a few left-hand notes (in this case, the fretted A, E, and G# notes on the sixth, fifth, and fourth strings, respectively) and experiment tapping at various points along the string with each pitch until you come up with a melody you like.

TRACK 56

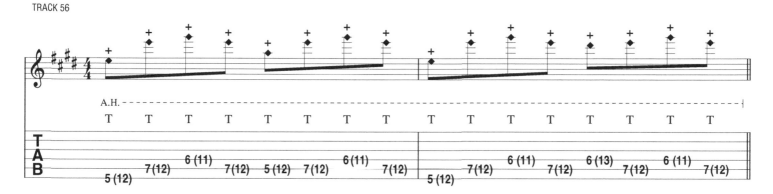

Lick #1

Our first lick here illustrates another important variation of the tapped harmonic—the *touch harmonic*. In measure 1, it isn't really necessary to tap the harmonic at the twentieth fret. Since the string is already in motion, and the octave harmonic is such a strong and easily sounding harmonic, you really only need to quickly touch the string at the twentieth fret. This will sound the harmonic clearly. You can tap it if you'd like, as this will probably produce a slightly louder harmonic, but you don't have to. Anytime you have a string in motion already on a lower fretted note, you have the option of using the touch harmonic or the tap harmonic for the first one. If you want to immediately play another harmonic, you'll need to tap from then on. In measure 2, we're tapping the fifteenth fret harmonic and then bending and releasing the note a whole step. The final two tap harmonics in this phrase will be tough to sound. You really need to whack the string to get them.

TRACK 57

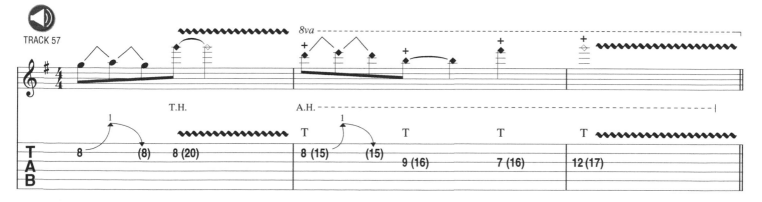

Lick #2

Lick #2 is another fun one because you get to hear a melody that seems to contradict what your left hand is doing. If you were to play just the left-hand notes here, you would hear a very standard pentatonic lick. But with the tap harmonics, a new (albeit still pentatonic) melody is created. This one is easy for your tapping hand because you're always tapping twelfth-fret harmonics.

TRACK 58

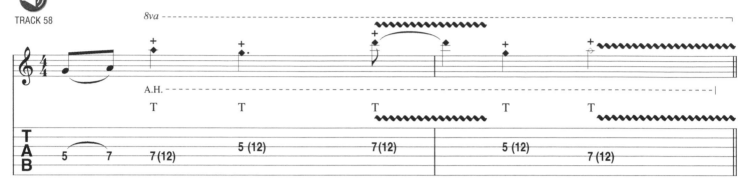

Chordal Tapping

In this technique, we're treating the guitar almost like a piano, using all of our left- and right-hand fingers to tap chords, melodies, or both simultaneously. Unlike most of the other techniques in this book, chordal tapping usually sounds best with a clean tone, so all of the notes are clearly audible. Don't be afraid to try it with a distorted tone, though. You just may not be able to hear more sophisticated harmonies as well.

Exercise #1

This first exercise introduces the technique in a D major progression of I–V–vi–IV–I. In the notation, the notes without numbers beside them are to be hammered with your left hand; the notes with numbers are to be tapped by the indicated right-hand finger. Note: it's a good idea to get into the habit of deadening the strings with the left hand behind the right-hand tapped notes when possible. This will prevent the simultaneous sounding of the intended tapped note and the note from the other side of the string (towards the nut). This isn't as apparent when playing through an amp, but try it without an amp and you'll hear this immediately. For example, in measure 1, after tapping the D and A notes with your left hand, allow the curvature of your first finger to lie across the strings and deaden them along the fifth fret. Repeat this procedure for each chord. This will ensure that only the intended notes are sounding.

TRACK 59

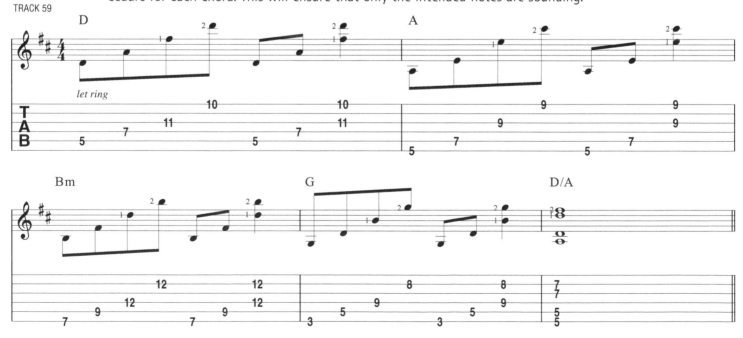

Exercise #2

Exercise #2 is a 12/8 example in G minor. In this exercise you'll get plenty of practice with simultaneously tapping chords with your right hand. The bass line remains the same for each of the two-measure phrases, so don't let the syncopation in beat 4 throw you off. It's pretty tough to cram all your fingers into the fifteenth fret in beats 4 of measures 3 and 4, so you may have to experiment with different angles to get all the notes to sound. If you have to omit one note, I would suggest omitting either the G note or the B♭ note, as the D is important to the E♭maj9 sound.

TRACK 60

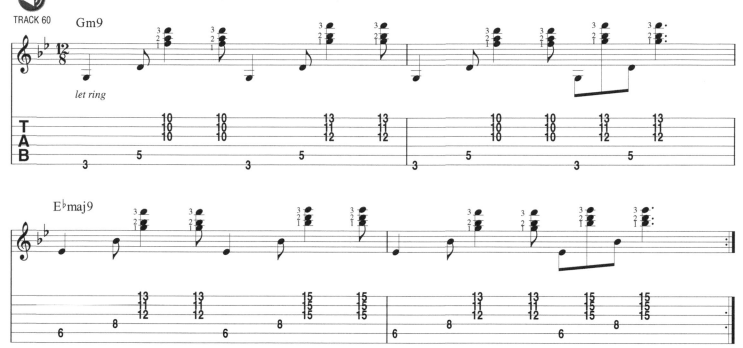

Lick #1

In this first lick, in Em, we're tapping 6ths in the right hand exclusively in the 3–1 string group. The left hand will hammer 5ths exclusively in measure 1, while in measure 2 we play a root/5th bass line with the inclusion of the 6th. In beat 2 of measure 1, we're tapping the E/G dyad and sliding up a whole step to F#/A. Measure 2 will require some independence between the hands, so be sure to work it out slowly at first.

TRACK 61

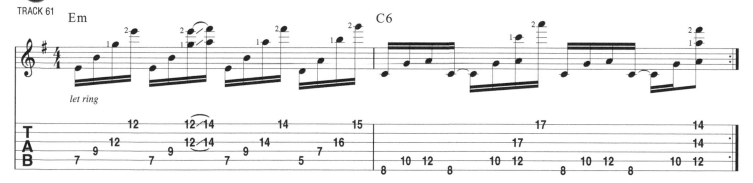

Lick #2

Lick #2 has a funky, Stevie Wonder-inspired feel to it. This one features two truly independent lines and will take a while to work up. Pay attention to the staccato marks; they're important in achieving the funk sound. Make sure that the bass line is prominent throughout. I suggest working out each individual voice first before attempting to put them together.

TRACK 62

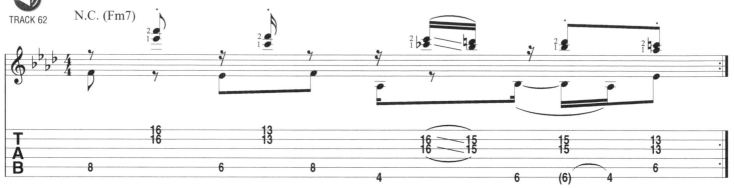

Style Applications

Slow Rock

Here we see a slow rock groove in C# minor. Melodies are stressed here throughout. We begin with a pick-up phrase that involves tapping the E note and sliding it down to D# before pulling it off to B. In beat 2, we tap a repeated E note for an interesting effect and slide it up to F#. The quick slide in beat 3 may take a little getting used to; make sure the rhythm is clear and the pitches are distinct.

TRACK 63

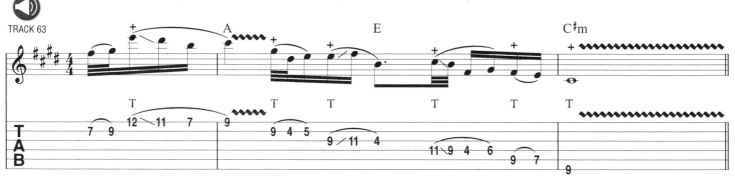

Rock

In this E minor lick, we begin with a hammer from G to A on the second string. Next, tap the D note at the fifteenth fret, bend it a whole step with your left hand, pull it off to the bent tenth fret (sounding the note B), release the bend to A, and pull off to G. In beat 4, tap the F# note, bend it up a half step to G, release it, and pull off to D. In measure 2, we're combing a tapped bend with a slide. Bend the tapped A up a whole step to B, release it back to A, then slide down to G and pull off to E.

TRACK 64

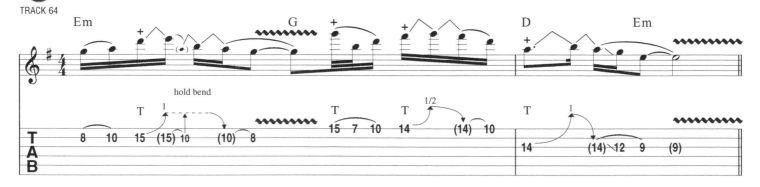

Ballad Rock

In this lick, we use tapped harmonics to play through a I–IV–vi–III–IV progression in E major. We begin on the G string in measure 1 tapping seven frets above (fret 14) the fretted D note, sounding the note A. After sliding our fret hand up a whole step, we tap again at fret 14 (this time five frets higher than the fretted note) and sound the E note. Shifting to the second string, we tap the fourteenth fret again while fretting the seventh and sound the C#, then tap the fourteenth fret while fretting the ninth, sounding the high G#. This note is bent and released a half step. In measure 2, we tap an octave above the G# note and bend and release by half steps. In beat 4, we begin with a good ol' fashioned normal tapping lick outlining G#7 and finish by tapping the sixteenth fret while fretting the ninth on the fourth string to sound the final F# note. For many of the harmonics in the first measure, you'll really need to experiment with finding the best spot on the string to tap for the harmonic to ring out.

TRACK 65

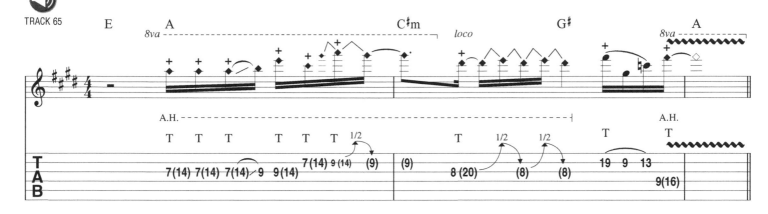

Funk Rock

With its sliding 4ths and 6ths, this chordal lick has a slight Motown flavor to it. This one really needs to be tackled as two independent parts, and each one needs to be learned separately before attempting to combine them. Notice that the bass line in each measure is very similar, with beat 2 marking the only significant difference. The Ab note in beat 3 of measure 1 lends a bluesy sound to the phrase. The bass slides in beats 4 of each measure are subtle but integral to the sound. Take this one slowly!

TRACK 66

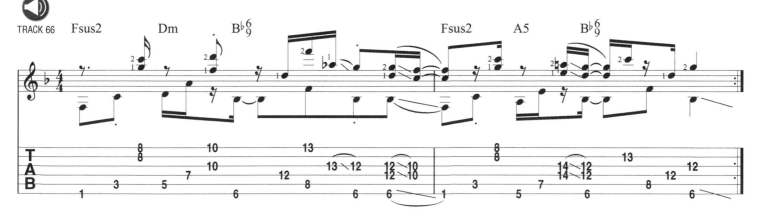

6 Multi-Fingered Tapping

Just when you thought you'd gotten a grip on the whole tapping thing, along comes multi-fingered tapping. In this technique, we're going to use the second, third, and fourth fingers of our right hand to extend the tapping possibilities. You may say, "Big deal. We already did that in the Chordal Tapping section." Ah, but this will be different. In this technique, you're required to treat your right hand much like your left hand, hammering on and pulling off notes in your *right hand.* A word of warning: your fingers are going to get sore!

Exercise #1

We begin with Exercise #1 on the low E string. I set the string into motion with a ghost pull-off from my right-hand first finger. You'll need to rotate your right hand so that it's perpendicular to the fretboard—forming somewhat of a mirror image of your left hand—in order to accurately perform the tapped E and G notes. Once you've tapped the G with your right-hand third finger, pull that off to your right-hand first finger on E (which should still be planted from the tap), then pull the E off to your left hand. The next measure is the same, except here we're tapping D and E with the first and second fingers of our right hand.

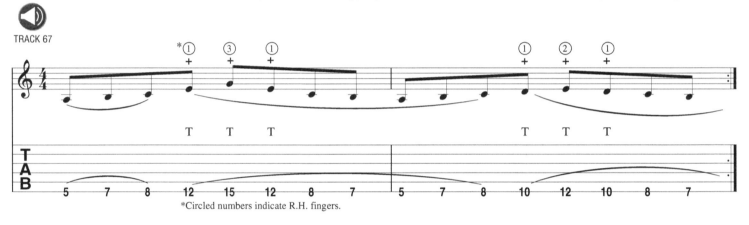

TRACK 67

*Circled numbers indicate R.H. fingers.

Some Notes on Muting ... Again

Well, now that you've probably gotten the hang of muting with the standard tapping technique, it's time to throw you a curve. Multi-fingered tapping presents some altogether new muting challenges. While some players get around this by using some sort of damping device that lightly touches the strings at the first fret (essentially muting any string that's not being played) you'll need to learn to mute on your own if you plan on incorporating any open strings into your multi-fingered licks. Besides, those things just kind of seem like cheating a little bit!

Essentially, muting with the multi-finger technique involves transferring the responsibility from your right hand to left hand several times within the same lick. While your right palm can handle all of the muting when tapping normally, this isn't practical when using other fingers of your right hand because of the arched position you'll need to use in order to reach the notes. We didn't need to worry about this in the first exercise because the example was performed entirely on the sixth string. I did that on purpose! I had to make it seem easy in order for you to want to give this technique a try. If you were to simply perform the rest of these multi-fingered licks with no regard for muting, the low strings would begin to make noise. If you're playing in A or E, this could end up sounding something like the black sheep of the bagpipe family. If you're playing in other keys, it usually just sounds plain ugly.

Lick #1

Lick #1 is performed entirely on the first string and is in the key of E minor. We begin with a standard tap and pull-off at the twelfth fret. At this point, your tapping hand should be in standard tapping position; i.e., it should be muting strings 2 through 6. As you hammer on to the D note from B, you'll need to change your right-hand position to access the F# and G notes. As you do this, lay your left-hand second finger (since it's not being used) across the strings to keep them quiet while you tap the F# and G notes. As you pull off the F# note to the B note, your right hand should move back into standard tapping position and mute the strings. Perform the same series of moves for the G and B tapped notes. Practice this very slowly, making sure that you're consistently muting the unwanted open strings at each and every point throughout the lick. If you spend the extra time getting this right in the beginning, it will become second nature.

TRACK 68

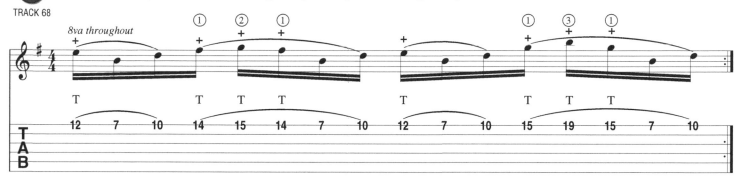

Exercise #2

Exercise #2 is in F major and is performed entirely on the fourth string. We begin by running up the F major pentatonic scale, tapping the C and D notes with our right-hand fingers 1 and 2. Again, as you transfer your right hand into position to tap the C and D notes, use your first finger to bridge across strings 5 and 6 to keep them quiet. I use the first finger here since it's played first and seems the most natural to me. In measure 2, we bring our right-hand fourth finger into play to reach the octave F. Hammering with your fourth finger is going to take some practice, but the coordination *will* eventually develop. In measures 3 and 4, we see the minor variation of this. Measure 4 is going to provide additional problems because you're required to tap from finger 3 of your right hand a whole step higher to finger 4! Start slow and be persistent!

TRACK 69

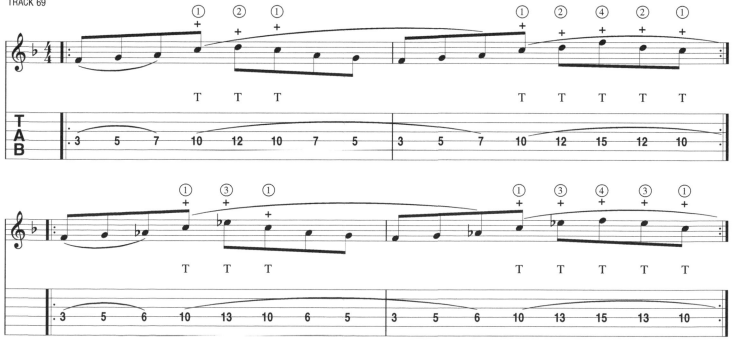

Lick #2

Ok. I can see that you're getting bored with these examples—they're just too easy. So, it's time to raise the bar. In Lick #2, we're not only using multi-fingered tapping, we're changing strings in the middle as well. We begin on the fourth string with a run up and down the A minor pentatonic scale, using fingers 1, 2, and 4 to tap the D, E, and G notes. In beats 3 and 4, we ascend as we did before up to D, but then we jump to the third string with fingers 2 and 4 of our right hand to tap A and C and pull back off to A. We finish off by tapping D with our first finger and pulling off to C and then A to start again. Listen closely when you're switching strings between taps to make sure the notes aren't ringing together.

TRACK 70

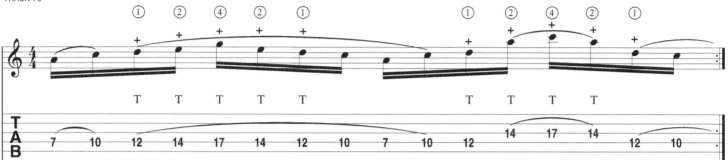

Exercise #3

I don't know if this happened to any of you, but when I was working out Lick #2, I would sometimes accidentally tap the second string with my fourth finger instead of the third string. Well, that gave me the idea for the next two examples. In Exercise #3, we develop the multi-string, multi-fingered technique by tapping up to each note of a G minor pentatonic scale on strings 3–1. We use a repeating Gm arpeggio figure on the fourth string (G and B♭ with fingers 1 and 4 of the left hand and D with finger 1 of the right hand) between each pentatonic note. After we reach the top G note, the multi-finger taps fall on notes of the G minor arpeggio for the descent. As far as muting goes, you can pretty much get away with leaving your right hand in arched position and leaving your left-hand second finger bridged across the low strings since it's not used at all.

TRACK 71

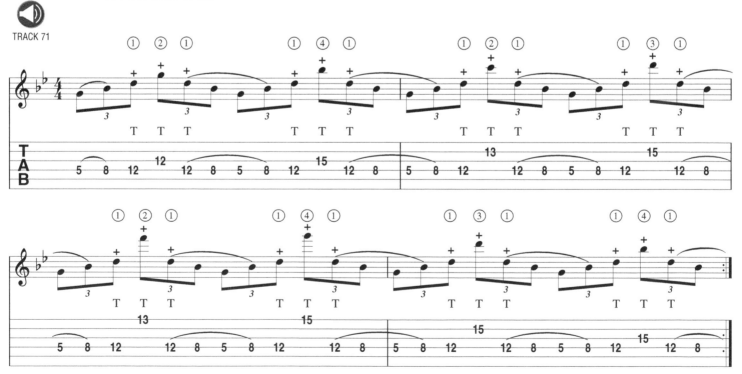

Lick #3

In Lick #3, we're essentially combining the approaches of Lick #2 and Exercise #3. The result is a fusion-sounding lick in G minor that, when played quickly, kind of sounds like something from a video game. In beats 1 and 2, you're required to tap up and down perfect 4ths with right-hand fingers 1, 2, and 3. This is followed in beat 2 with a tap and pull-off with fingers 2 and 4 of your right hand. In beats 1 and 2 of measure 2 we use fingers 1, 2, and 4 of our right hand to tap up and down a minor 7th and a perfect 5th interval. In beats 3 and 4, we see an alternative fingering to the problem we encountered at the end of Exercise #2 (in F minor). There we tapped a minor 3rd from our first finger to our third, and continued to tap a major 2nd from our third finger to our fourth all on the D string. In this variation, we begin the same way by tapping a minor 3rd from first to third finger, but then we use our first finger to tap the tonic note on the G string. We continue back down by tapping again on the D string with our third finger and pulling off to our first. If the whole-step tap/pull-off move with fingers 3 and 4 is too difficult, you may find this method a little easier. Of course, if you're on the high E string, you don't have a choice. In between the right-hand taps is the same G minor arpeggio motif that we saw in Exercise #3.

TRACK 72

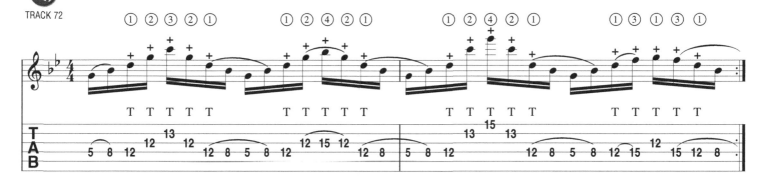

Exercise #4

Exercise #4 makes use of all four fingers of your right hand in the same phrase. This one is designed to begin coordinating your right-hand fingers so they'll be able to conform to different fret patterns. Just as you sometimes have to stretch with your left hand to access certain notes or shapes, so will you with your right hand. In measure 1, we begin ascending up the E major scale. As your fourth finger (left hand) plays G#, bridge your first finger across all the strings to keep them quiet. In beat 2 we tap up the 5th, 6th, 7th, and octave degrees of the scale and then pull off back down. It's going to take some time to develop the strength and precision needed here. You're asking your right hand to do something it's never done, and it's going to give you lots of grief for it. In measure 2, we see the minor variation of this. A good way to practice these is to isolate the right-hand parts and loop them. Use your left hand to mute the strings, and just play B–C#–D#–E–D#–C# over and over until you get the hang of it. Then play the minor variation (B–C–D–E–D–C) until you get that. Once you're comfortable with the right-hand section, begin to incorporate the left hand for the full effect. Note: If you find yourself blazing through this exercise flawlessly at 160 bpm in a day or so, then you should probably get out more. Maybe you should go see a movie or something.

TRACK 73

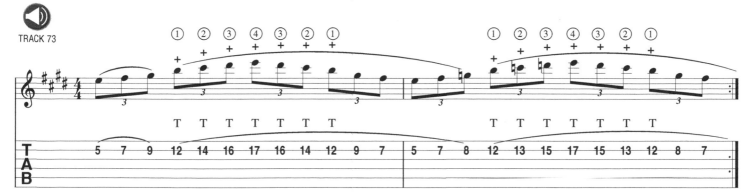

Lick #4

In Lick #4, we have a lick performed entirely on the second string based on the E minor hexatonic scale (E–F#–G–A–B–D). This one makes use of all four of your right hand fingers as well, but not at the same time. You should begin with your right hand palm muting strings 3–6. After the initial ascent from G to B in beat 1, your left-hand first finger should stay bridged across the strings the whole time until the end of beat 4 when the lick is ready to repeat. At this point, use your right-hand palm to take over the muting once more.

TRACK 74

Style Applications

Hard Rock

This first example in E minor demonstrates how the multi-fingered technique can be used to create quick, fluid, ascending sequences all on one string. This one is performed entirely on the D string and doesn't require any big right-hand stretches, so it shouldn't pose too many problems in that area—especially if you've mastered the previous examples. The only problems you'll have to concentrate on here are position shifts. Every two beats, we slide up with our left hand into a new position, so you'll have to learn to quickly change positions with both hands.

TRACK 75

Rock

Here we find an E major example that is similar in concept to Exercise #3. We use a pedaling E major scale figure in the left hand in between taps on the second and first strings. Beat 3 will likely pose the biggest problem; getting your fourth finger out there on its own to reach the G# will take a bit of practice. In beat 4, we slide down a half step momentarily into fourth position and finish off with a standard tapping lick incorporating the open high E string.

TRACK 76

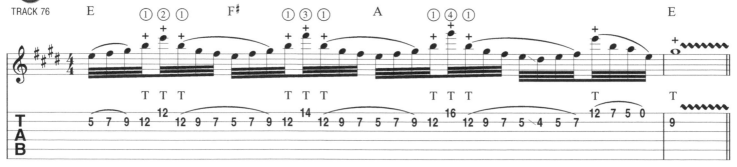

7 Combining Techniques

With the previous chapter, I'm sure some of you realized just how far this tapping thing can go. When you combine the multi-fingered tapping idea with some of the other ideas from earlier chapters, you really are limited only by your imagination. This chapter is intended to provide a brief glimpse into some of the possibilities that arise when you throw all these ideas together into one lick.

Lick #1

Lick #1, in G major, combines the multi-fingered technique with the tapped bend and tapped slide techniques. After tapping onto the high G with the fourth finger, use your left hand to bend up to A and re-lease back down to G. In beat 3, we use the right hand to play a short two-note sequence before finishing off with a tapped slide in beat 4.

TRACK 77

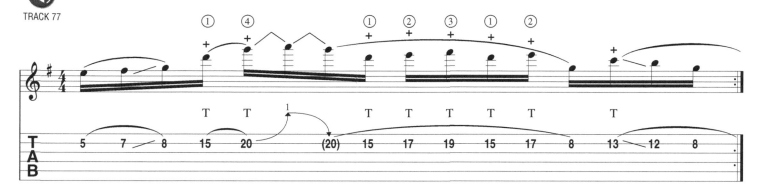

Lick #2

In Lick #2, we combine the tapped bend and tapped bend-and-slide with the multi-fingered technique. Begin with the left-hand hammer and bend. While holding the bend, perform the following moves: Tap fret 12 with your first finger and slide up a whole step to fret 14. Next, tap fret 16 with your second finger, pull off to your first finger at fret 14, and pull that off to your left hand pre-bent at fret 9. Tap fret 14 with your first finger, release the left-hand bend, slide your first finger down a half step to fret 13, and pull off to your left hand on fret 9. Finally, tap fret 14 with your second finger, pull off to your right-hand first finger at fret 13, pull off to your left-hand third finger at fret 9, and tap fret 11 withyour left-hand first finger. The biggest problem you will probably encounter here is not accidentally sounding the D string when you're tapping the bent G string. There's little room for error.

TRACK 78

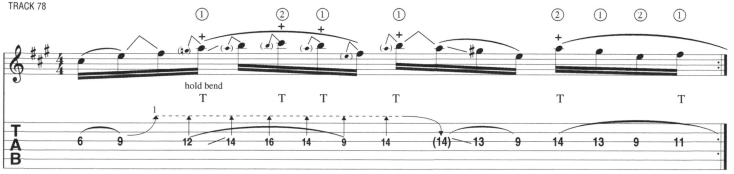

43

Lick #3

Lick #3 runs up a B♭ major scale to the 9th and back down all on the G string. Begin by sliding and hammering in your left hand up the E♭ and tapping onto the F with your first finger. Bend the tapped note up a whole step; this bend will be held until beat 3 of measure 2. Next, slide the tapped note up a whole step, tap fret 13 with your second finger, tap fret 15 with your third finger, pull off to your second finger at fret 13, and pull off to your first finger at fret 12. Slide your first finger down to fret 10, release the bend (sounding an F note), and pull off to your left hand for the final descent.

TRACK 79

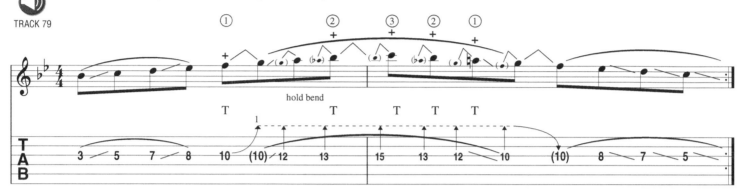

Lick #4

In Lick #4, we're combining the ascending tap concept, tapped bends, tapped slides, and multi-fingered tapping. The tonality of this lick is A Mixolydian (A–B–C♯–D–E–F♯–G), and we begin on the fourth string with some left-hand hammer-ons. After tapping the G note at the end of beat 1, I use my right-hand third finger to pluck the F♯ note on string 2. The tapped bend in beat 2 should seem relatively tame by now. In beat 3 we use our first and third fingers to tap on strings 2 and 1, including a tapped slide from C♯ to C♮ for a bluesy effect. At the beginning of measure 2, tap F♯ at fret 14 with your first finger, bend up a half step to G with your left hand, tap fret 16 with your third finger (sounding the note A), pull off to your first finger at fret 14 (sounding G), and release the bend back to F♯. We finish things off in beat 3 with a tapped E with your third finger pulling off to C♯ with your first finger, which is pulled off to the final A note in your left hand.

TRACK 80

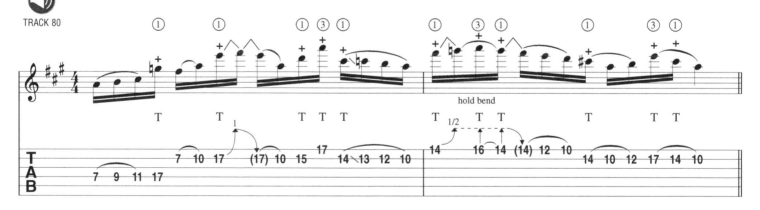

Hopefully by now you're beginning to see the limitless potential that exists when all of these techniques are combined. These four licks merely scratch the surface of possibilities. I encourage you to experiment and come up with your own licks using the various techniques and combinations available. You're not going to run out of ideas—I guarantee you!

8 Putting It All Together

Ok. It's time to see how all these concepts can be used in some actual full-length solos. In this chapter, we'll look at four different solos that use various tapping techniques exclusively, proving that all is not lost if you happen to drop your pick right before your solo! Remember that, by using the balance control on your stereo, you can isolate just the lead track for closer study, or, you can completely remove the lead track and jam along with the rhythm tracks by yourself.

After you've got the written solos down, try coming up with your own solos over the rhythm tracks and record them if you have the means. Listening back to yourself is one of the best teachers you can ever have. If you're having trouble coming up with ideas, try transposing some of your favorite licks from this book to the key of the rhythm track and see if you can fit them in somewhere as a starting point.

Solo #1
Minor Blues

Our first solo is played over a minor blues in C with a shuffle feel. The first chorus is comprised entirely of the chordal tapping technique played with a clean tone. I walk a bass line with my left hand while using my right hand to tap chords and occasionally melodies. This is simulating what a combined bass and rhythm guitar part might sound like over this type of groove. Notice that, with a few exceptions, the left-hand part remains mostly in fifth position. This makes the job a bit easier, since you're really only having to concentrate on watching the right hand.

In the second chorus, I switch to a distorted tone and begin to play lead. Phrasing-wise, I'm stressing melodies and using a wide range, thinking more along the lines of a sax player rather than typical guitar phrasing. The phrase leading into the second chorus is based on the C Dorian mode (measure 11) and the C harmonic minor scale (measure 12). In measure 14, we use tapped slides to create an angular pentatonic sequence. Multi-fingered tapping is employed in measure 15 to outline a Gm7 arpeggio. Over the Cm7 chord, this results in a Cm11 tonality. The lick in measure 16 treats the C as a dominant, with the presence of E♮ leading into the following F minor chord. Measure 18 combines the tapped bend technique with a tapped slide for a melodic highlight. We use the ascending tap concept in measure 20, repeating the same lick an octave higher. The phrase in measure 22 is based on the G whole tone scale, which is tailor made for the G+7 chord. We wrap things up in measure 23 with a run down the C blues scale and end on the 9th (D).

TRACK 81

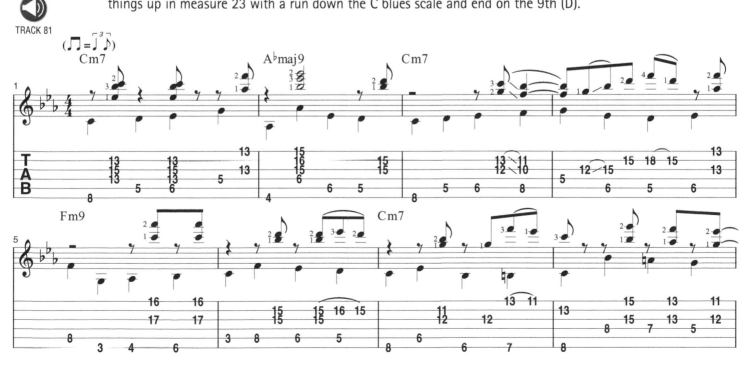

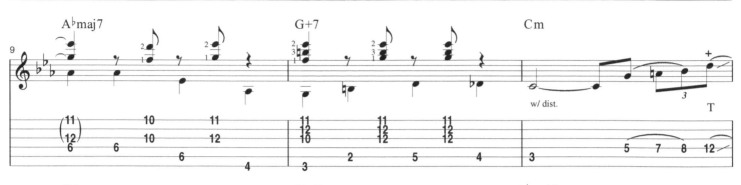

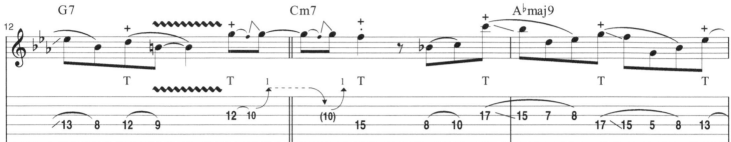

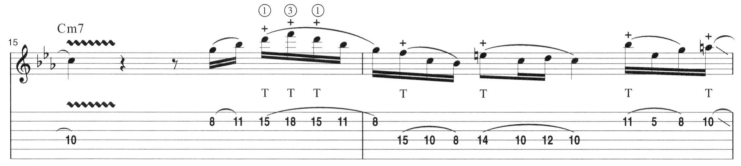

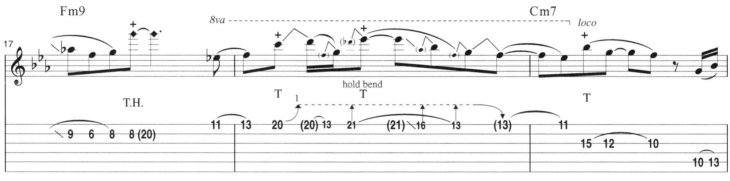

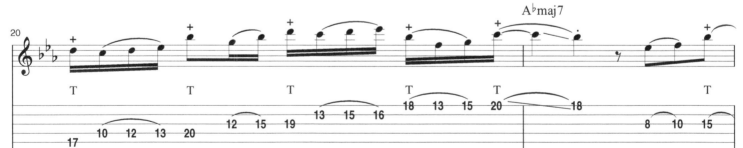

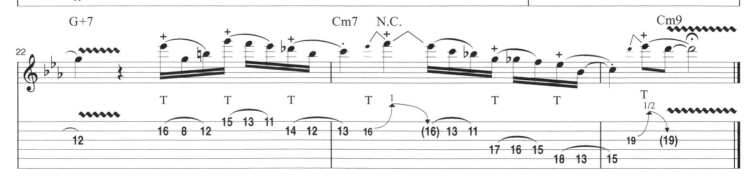

Solo #2
Bright Rock

Our second solo is played over a bright rock groove in A major. We begin in measures 1–4 using the ascending tap concept with imitative phrasing. In measure 4, we tap fret 19, bend it a whole step (with our left-hand third finger on fret 17), slide up a half step to fret 20, pull it off to our left hand at fret 17, then release the bend. Note the use of D# in measure 8; this is the 3rd of the B chord. In measure 9, we make use of string skipping to tap down a Dmaj7 arpeggio. This is contrasted in measure 10 with an ascending run up F# minor pentatonic with some repeated notes. Measures 13 and 14 make use of string skipping again, and in beats 3 and 4 of measure 14 we see a pedal point lick with the tonic note (A) acting as the pedal. We close out the solo in measures 15 and 16 with a multi-finger, multi-string lick that implies an Esus4–E progression.

TRACK 82

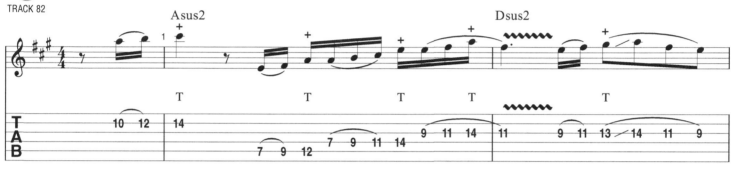

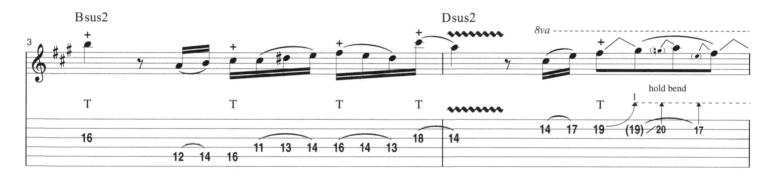

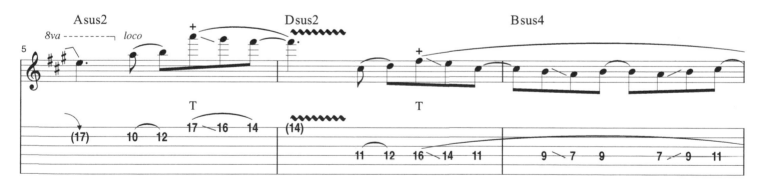

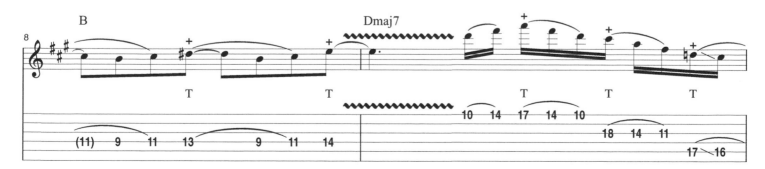

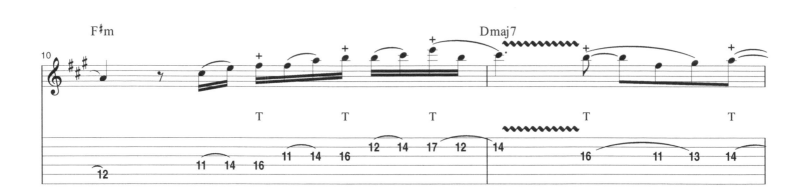

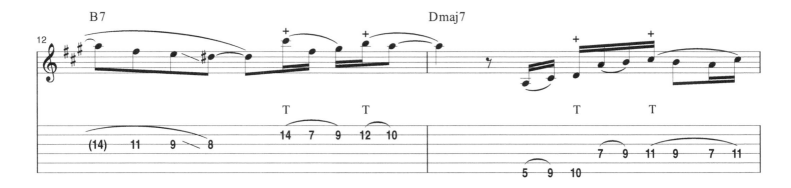

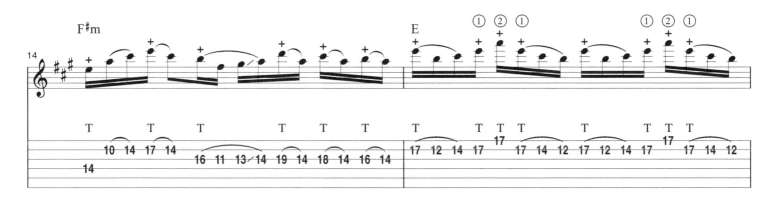

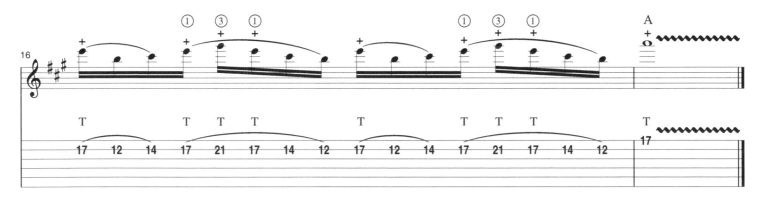

Solo #3
Hard Rock

Here's a typical hard rock groove in D minor—a perfect vehicle with which to flaunt your tapping chops. This one is pretty much all about flash. In fact, we're playing straight sixteenth notes all the way until measure 12. We open with some repeated figures in measures 1–4, all played on the high E string. Make sure you're getting all the notes clean and in time here. It's easy to sort of slop through these kinds of phrases; you want to make sure every note is heard and that you're not rushing through parts and dragging through others. In measures 5 and 6, we use the D minor hexatonic scale (D–E–F–G–A–C) to descend through a sequence on the first four strings. This phrase is syncopated throughout, so watch the rhythm again. In measure 7, we use the ascending tap concept to run up the scale over the Csus2 chord. Notice that the first notes of each beat outline the Csus2 chord. Measure 8 begins a lick that is developed further in the second chorus beginning in measure 9. Here we use tapped bends to lend a synthesizer sound to the lick; it sounds similar to a phrase manipulated by the pitch wheel. In measures 11 and 12, we descend straight through the scale for two octaves with four notes per string. Notice that the tapped note is not on the downbeat; it's on the upbeat, forcing you to really concentrate on the timing. Measure 13 makes use of the multi-fingered, multi-string technique, as does the cadenza in measures 15 and 16.

TRACK 83

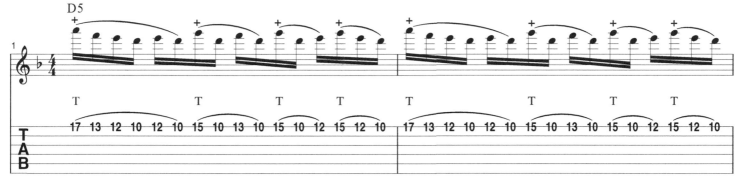

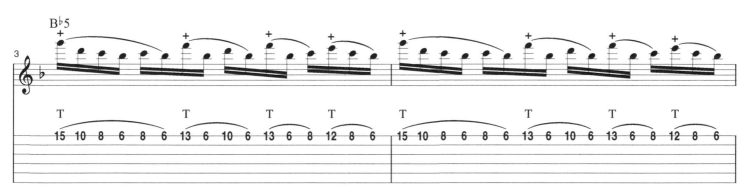

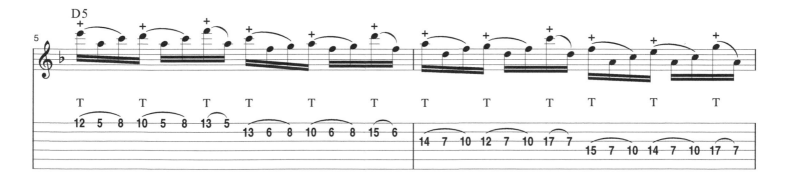

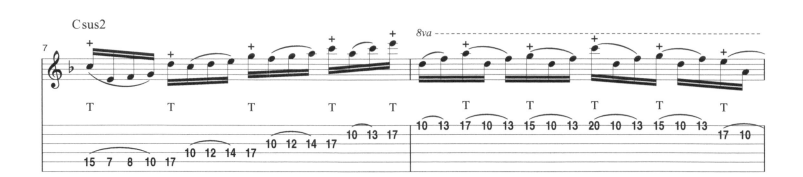

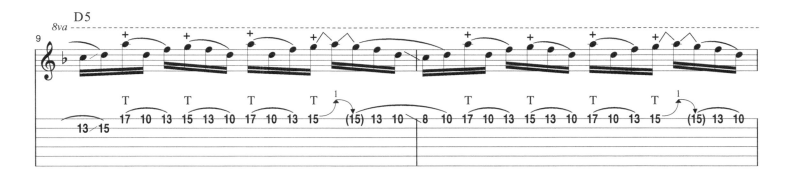

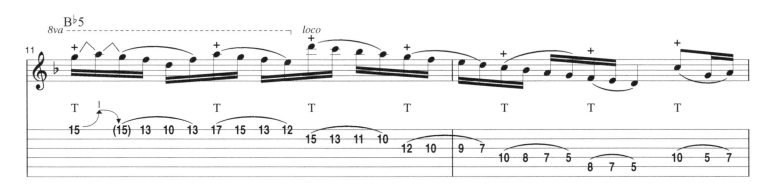

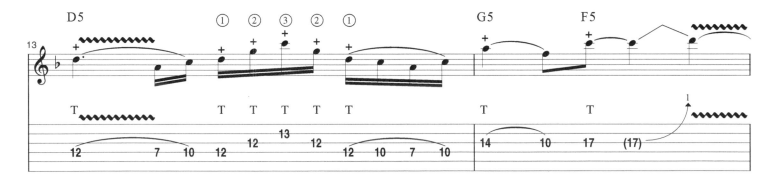

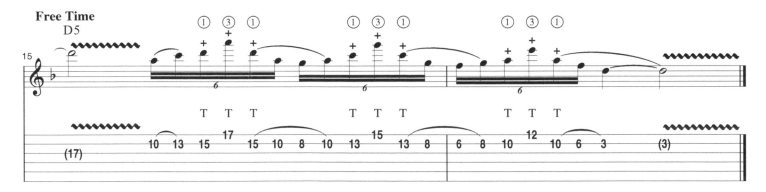

Solo #4
12/8 Ballad

Our last solo is over a 12/8 groove in G major. There are two notable non-diatonic chords, Fadd9 and Aadd9, and each one is given specific melodic treatment. We open things up in measures 1 and 2 with some sparse melodic statements making use of tapped slides and bends. Notice the presence of F♮ coinciding with the Fadd9 chord in measure 2. Measures 3 and 4 contain several scalar flurries that descend in pitch to target the A chord. Notice that beat 1 of measure 4 descends down an A9 arpeggio. Multi-fingered tapping is briefly employed at the end of the measure over the C chord. Measure 5 contains a multi-fingered monster lick consisting of straight thirty-second notes. This is contrasted in measure 6 with some melodies making use of tapped harmonics and touch harmonics. You really have to be precise to hit the tapped harmonic at fret 22. We use multi-fingered tapping again in measure 7 to play a major pentatonic lick on string 2 and make use of string skipping in beats 3 and 4 to outline notes of the Em9 and C chords. Measure 8 includes the C♯ note again over the Aadd9 chord with a brief use of the second right-hand finger on string 2. In beats 3 and 4 of the same measure, we include the note B♭ for a bluesy sound over the C chord. We wrap things up in measure 10 with an ascending tap lick with a repeated note that resolves on the tonic (G).

TRACK 84

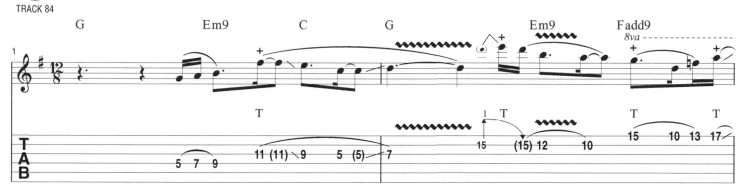

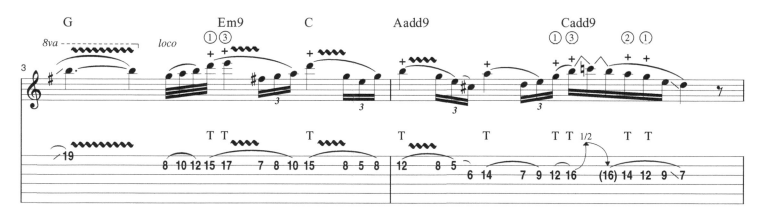

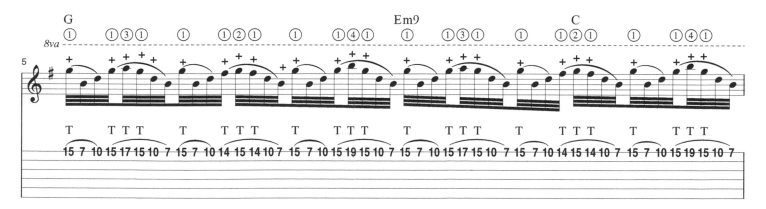

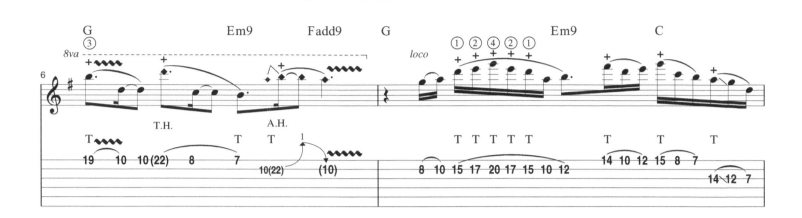

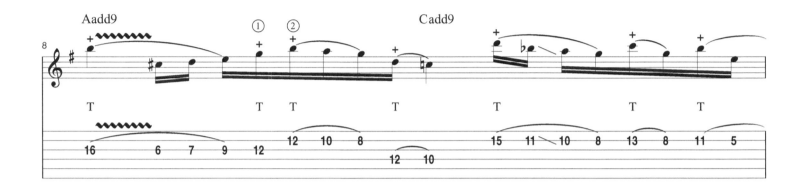

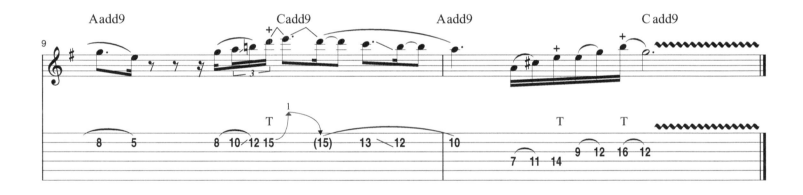

Afterword

I hope I've managed to shed some new light on tapping technique and that you've found the examples in this book to be inspiring and useful. As I mentioned a few times already, you'll be hard pressed to ever run out of ideas if you make use of all the techniques presented here. Listen to your favorite players to see if you can identify some of them, and try playing some of the licks in this book with an alternate technique—in other words, try replacing a tapped slide with a tapped bend, or vice versa. Many times, it's this sort of experimentation that can help you find your own style. Good luck and have fun!

About the Author

Chad Johnson studied music at the University of North Texas from 1990–1995. In 1998, he became a senior music editor for iSong.com, an internet-based company that produced instructional guitar-based CDs. After leaving iSong.com in 2000, he began editing, proofing, and authoring books for Hal Leonard. *Guitar Tapping* is the fifth book Chad has written for Hal Leonard Corporation. His other books include *7-String Guitar Chord Book, Alternate Tuning Chord Dictionary, Chops Builder for Guitar,* and *Pentatonic Scales for Guitar.* Currently, Chad resides in Plano, TX, and keeps busy writing, editing, composing, and recording. For correspondence, write to: chadljohnson@hotmail.com.

Guitar Notation Legend

Guitar Music can be notated three different ways: on a *musical staff*, in *tablature*, and in *rhythm slashes*.

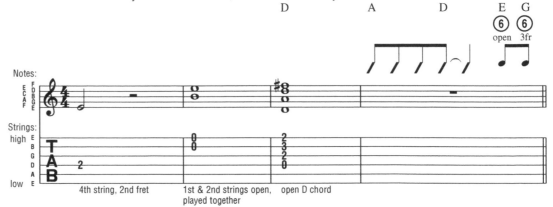

RHYTHM SLASHES are written above the staff. Strum chords in the rhythm indicated. Use the chord diagrams found at the top of the first page of the transcription for the appropriate chord voicings. Round noteheads indicate single notes.

THE MUSICAL STAFF shows pitches and rhythms and is divided by bar lines into measures. Pitches are named after the first seven letters of the alphabet.

TABLATURE graphically represents the guitar fingerboard. Each horizontal line represents a string, and each number represents a fret.

HALF-STEP BEND: Strike the note and bend up 1/2 step.

WHOLE-STEP BEND: Strike the note and bend up one step.

GRACE NOTE BEND: Strike the note and immediately bend up as indicated.

SLIGHT (MICROTONE) BEND: Strike the note and bend up 1/4 step.

BEND AND RELEASE: Strike the note and bend up as indicated, then release back to the original note. Only the first note is struck.

PRE-BEND: Bend the note as indicated, then strike it.

VIBRATO: The string is vibrated by rapidly bending and releasing the note with the fretting hand.

WIDE VIBRATO: The pitch is varied to a greater degree by vibrating with the fretting hand.

HAMMER-ON: Strike the first (lower) note with one finger, then sound the higher note (on the same string) with another finger by fretting it without picking.

PULL-OFF: Place both fingers on the notes to be sounded. Strike the first note and without picking, pull the finger off to sound the second (lower) note.

LEGATO SLIDE: Strike the first note and then slide the same fret-hand finger up or down to the second note. The second note is not struck.

SHIFT SLIDE: Same as legato slide, except the second note is struck.

TRILL: Very rapidly alternate between the notes indicated by continuously hammering on and pulling off.

TAPPING: Hammer ("tap") the fret indicated with the pick-hand index or middle finger and pull off to the note fretted by the fret hand.

NATURAL HARMONIC: Strike the note while the fret-hand lightly touches the string directly over the fret indicated.

PINCH HARMONIC: The note is fretted normally and a harmonic is produced by adding the edge of the thumb or the tip of the index finger of the pick hand to the normal pick attack.

PICK SCRAPE: The edge of the pick is rubbed down (or up) the string, producing a scratchy sound.

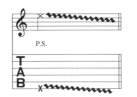

MUFFLED STRINGS: A percussive sound is produced by laying the fret hand across the string(s) without depressing, and striking them with the pick hand.

PALM MUTING: The note is partially muted by the pick hand lightly touching the string(s) just before the bridge.

RAKE: Drag the pick across the strings indicated with a single motion.

TREMOLO PICKING: The note is picked as rapidly and continuously as possible.

VIBRATO BAR DIVE AND RETURN: The pitch of the note or chord is dropped a specified number of steps (in rhythm) then returned to the original pitch.

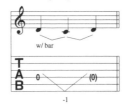

VIBRATO BAR SCOOP: Depress the bar just before striking the note, then quickly release the bar.

VIBRATO BAR DIP: Strike the note and then immediately drop a specified number of steps, then release back to the original pitch.

Get Better at Guitar

...with these Great Guitar Instruction Books from Hal Leonard!

101 GUITAR TIPS
INCLUDES TAB
STUFF ALL THE PROS KNOW AND USE

by Adam St. James
This book contains invaluable guidance on everything from scales and music theory to truss rod adjustments, proper recording studio set-ups, and much more.

00695737 Book/Online Audio $17.99

AMAZING PHRASING
INCLUDES TAB

by Tom Kolb
This book/audio pack explores all the main components necessary for crafting well-balanced rhythmic and melodic phrases. It also explains how these phrases are put together to form cohesive solos. The companion audio contains 89 demo tracks, most with full-band backing.

00695583 Book/Online Audio $22.99

ARPEGGIOS FOR THE MODERN GUITARIST
INCLUDES TAB

by Tom Kolb
Using this no-nonsense book with online audio, guitarists will learn to apply and execute all types of arpeggio forms using a variety of techniques, including alternate picking, sweep picking, tapping, string skipping, and legato.

00695862 Book/Online Audio $22.99

BLUES YOU CAN USE

by John Ganapes
This comprehensive source for learning blues guitar is designed to develop both your lead and rhythm playing. Includes: 21 complete solos • blues chords, progressions and riffs • turnarounds • movable scales and soloing techniques • string bending • utilizing the entire fingerboard • and more.

00142420 Book/Online Media.................$22.99

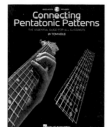

CONNECTING PENTATONIC PATTERNS
INCLUDES TAB

by Tom Kolb
If you've been finding yourself trapped in the pentatonic box, this book is for you! This hands-on book with online audio offers examples for guitar players of all levels, from beginner to advanced. Study this book faithfully, and soon you'll be soloing all over the neck with the greatest of ease.

00696445 Book/Online Audio $24.99

FRETBOARD MASTERY
INCLUDES TAB

by Troy Stetina
Untangle the mysterious regions of the guitar fretboard and unlock your potential. This book familiarizes you with all the shapes you need to know by applying them in real musical examples, thereby reinforcing and reaffirming your newfound knowledge.

00695331 Book/Online Audio $22.99

GUITAR AEROBICS
INCLUDES TAB

by Troy Nelson
Here is a daily dose of guitar "vitamins" to keep your chops fine tuned! Musical styles include rock, blues, jazz, metal, country, and funk. Techniques taught include alternate picking, arpeggios, sweep picking, string skipping, legato, string bending, and rhythm guitar.

00695946 Book/Online Audio $24.99

GUITAR CLUES
INCLUDES TAB
OPERATION PENTATONIC

by Greg Koch
Whether you're new to improvising or have been doing it for a while, this book/audio pack will provide loads of delicious licks and tricks that you can use right away, from volume swells and chicken pickin' to intervallic and chordal ideas.

00695827 Book/Online Audio $19.99

PAT METHENY – GUITAR ETUDES
INCLUDES TAB

Over the years, in many master classes and workshops around the world, Pat has demonstrated the kind of daily workout he puts himself through. This book includes a collection of 14 guitar etudes he created to help you limber up, improve picking technique and build finger independence.

00696587.................$17.99

PICTURE CHORD ENCYCLOPEDIA

This comprehensive guitar chord resource for all playing styles and levels features five voicings of 44 chord qualities for all twelve keys – 2,640 chords in all! For each, there is a clearly illustrated chord frame, as well as *an actual photo* of the chord being played!.

00695224.................$22.99

RHYTHM GUITAR 365
INCLUDES TAB

by Troy Nelson
This book provides 365 exercises – one for every day of the year! – to keep your rhythm chops fine tuned. Topics covered include: chord theory; the fundamentals of rhythm; fingerpicking; strum patterns; diatonic and non-diatonic progressions; triads; major and minor keys; and more.

00103627 Book/Online Audio $27.99

SCALE CHORD RELATIONSHIPS
INCLUDES TAB

by Michael Mueller & Jeff Schroedl
This book/audio pack explains how to: recognize keys • analyze chord progressions • use the modes • play over nondiatonic harmony • use harmonic and melodic minor scales • use symmetrical scales • incorporate exotic scales • and much more!

00695563 Book/Online Audio $17.99

SPEED MECHANICS FOR LEAD GUITAR
INCLUDES TAB

by Troy Stetina
Take your playing to the stratosphere with this advanced lead book which will help you develop speed and precision in today's explosive playing styles. Learn the fastest ways to achieve speed and control, secrets to make your practice time really count, and how to open your ears and make your musical ideas more solid and tangible.

00699323 Book/Online Audio $22.99

TOTAL ROCK GUITAR
INCLUDES TAB

by Troy Stetina
This comprehensive source for learning rock guitar is designed to develop both lead and rhythm playing. It covers: getting a tone that rocks • open chords, power chords and barre chords • riffs, scales and licks • string bending, strumming, and harmonics • and more.

00695246 Book/Online Audio $22.99

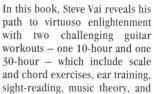

Guitar World Presents
INCLUDES TAB

STEVE VAI'S GUITAR WORKOUT

In this book, Steve Vai reveals his path to virtuoso enlightenment with two challenging guitar workouts – one 10-hour and one 30-hour – which include scale and chord exercises, ear training, sight-reading, music theory, and much more.

00119643.................$16.99

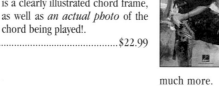
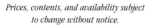